German Uniforms of the Third Reich 1933–1945

In color

by
BRIAN LEIGH DAVIS

illustrated by
PIERRE TURNER

ARCO PUBLISHING, INC.
New York

Published by Arco Publishing, Inc.
219 Park Avenue South, New York, N.Y. 10003

Printed in Singapore

Library of Congress Cataloging in Publication Data

Davis, Brian L
German uniforms of the Third Reich, 1933–1945.

Includes Index
1. Germany. Wehrmacht – Uniforms.
I. Turner, Pierre, joint author. II. Title.
UC485.G3D33   355.1'4'0943   80–77
ISBN 0-668-04938-3 (Cloth Edition)
ISBN 0-668-04940-5 (Paper Edition)

To my Mother

Contents

Organizations and Individuals   iv

Introduction and Acknowledgements   7

The Political Leadership Hierarchy
and the National Socialist
German Workers Party—NSDAP   12

Colour Plates   17

Plate Descriptions   97

Chart of Comparative Ranks   219

List of Abbreviations   224

Organizations and Individuals

	Figure Numbers
Der Führer, Adolf Hitler	1–3
Politischer Leiter der NSDAP	4–15
Stab der Ordensburg Vogelsang	13
Rudolf Hess, 5; Robert Ley, 10	
Sturmabteilung	16–17, 29
SA-Wehrmannschaft	16
Hilfspolizei der Gruppe Berlin-Brandenburg	19
Feldjägerkorps in Prussia	20
Stabswache Göring	21
SA-Standarte 'Feldherrnhalle'	26
Ernst Rohm, 17; Viktor Lutze, 23	
Marine-SA	28, 30
Nationalsozialistische Kraftfahrkorps	31–36
II. Marine-Brigade Ehrhardt	37
Stahlhelm	38, 39
Allgemeine-SS	40–48
Heinrich Himmler, 41; Reinhard Heydrich, 44	
SS-Verfügungstruppe	49–51
Hitler-Jugend	52–57
Flakhelfer der HJ	55
HJ-Freiwillige Feuerschutzhelfer	56
HJ-Streifendienst	57
Artur Axmann, 52	
Marine-Hitler-Jugend	58–60
Bund Deutsche Mädel	61–63, 236
Jutta Rüdiger, 62	
Deutsche Jungvolk	64–66
Freiwillige Arbeitsdienst	67–69
Reichsarbeitsdienst	70–76

Konstantin Hierl, 74

Reichsarbeitsdienst der Weiblichen Jugend 77–81

Deutsche Arbeitsfront 79–81

Nationalsozialistische Fliegerkorps 82–84

National Politische Erziehungsanstalt 85–87

Heer 88–108

Gerd von Rundstedt, 88; Generalleutnant
Siefert, 89; Wilhelm Keitel, 91.

Nachrichtenhelferinnen des Heeres 106–108

Kriegsmarine 109–120

Karl Dönitz, 109; Kapitänleutnant Lemp, 118;
Kapitän zur See Freymadel, 119.

Kriegsmarine-Artillerie 121–123

Deutscher Luftsport-Verband 124–126

Reichsmarschall Hermann Göring 127–129

Luftwaffe 130–138, 141, 142

Division 'Hermann Göring' 139

Legion Condor 140

Fallschirmjäger 143, 144, 146

Brigade 'Hermann Göring' 145

Luftwaffe Feld-Divisionen 147

Flakwaffenhelferinnen 148

SS-Helferinnen 149

Luftnachrichten-Helferinnen 150

Waffen-SS 151–162

Verkehrspolizei 163

Schutzpolizei des Reiches 164, 165

Motorisierten Gendarmerie 166, 178

Marine-Küsten-Polizei 167

Gendarmerie 168

Hochgebirgs Gendarmerie 169

Ordnungspolizei, Alfred Wünnenberg 170

Feuerschutzpolizei 171

Wasserschutzpolizei 172

Zollbeamten 173

Polizei-Regimenter 174

Bahnschutzpolizei 175

Kasernierte Polizei 177, 180
Verwaltungspolizei 179
Landespolizeigruppe 'General Göring' 181
Strafanstaltsbeamten 182
Polizeihelferinnen 183
Volkssturm 184–186
Diplomatisches Korps, Regierungs, Staats und
  Ministerial Beamten 187–192
  Joachim von Ribbentrop, 187–189;
  Reichspräsidialrat Kiewitz, 190; Otto Meissner, 191.
Ostbeamten 193, 194
Baudienst in Generalgouvernement 195
Reichsluftschutzbund 196–198
  von Roques, 197.
Sicherheits und Hilfsdienst 199, 200
Luftschutz Warndienst 201
Werkschutzpolizei 202–204
Deutsches Rotes Kreuz 205–210
Organisation Todt 211–213, 215
  Albert Speer, 212
Technische Nothilfe 176, 214, 217–219
  Hans Weinreich, 176
Transportkorps Speer 216
Deutsche Jägerschaft 220, 222
Deutschen Falkenordens 221
NS-Kriegsopferversorgung 223
NS-Reichskriegerbund 224
Deutsche Kolonialkriegerbund 225
Deutsche Reichsbahn 226–231
Deutsche Reichspost 232, 234
Postschutz 233
Verkehrsgesellschaften 235, 237
Deutsche Bergmänner 238–240

Introduction and Acknowledgements

In this book I have attempted to illustrate and explain just some of the many uniforms and items of official clothing together with their related insignia and accoutrements that were worn by Germans within Germany at one time or other both before and during the period of German history known as the Third Reich.

It has been my decision to divide the colour plates and the corresponding text into three general areas:

1) Those uniforms worn by the members of the National Socialist Party and its affiliated organisations,

2) Those formations that could be considered as having a fighting or police-like function and

3) Those bodies of officials who governed, administered or supervised everyday functions.

All uniformed organisations were issued with, or in the case of the officer classes, purchased for themselves, uniforms for general service wear. A number of formations wore specially produced uniforms that were made exclusively for parades, gala occasions, evening wear or special functions. Others who did not possess these special uniforms made do with a superior quality service uniform to which were added items of insignia or dress decorations that transformed their service uniform into a form of parade dress, evening wear or walking-out uniform. Most organisations had some form of work clothing or fatigue dress. Sports clothing (track suits, sports kit or swimming gear) was issued kit for all.

Other items worn were greatcoats, rain capes, cloaks, top coats, frock coats, raincoats and leather coats. Finally there was specialist clothing and protective garments provided for

7

those persons whose function required their wearing such things.

The uniformed garments themselves were fairly consistent. For normal purposes men of all formations wore jackets and tunics, shirts and blouses, trousers, breeches or shorts, greatcoats and leather coats, frock-coats, rain capes and rain coats or cloaks. Their heads were covered by peaked caps, side caps, berets, kepis or steel helmets. They wore leather high boots, marching boots, ankle boots or shoes. Women for their part were dressed in jackets and skirts, blouses or slacks and dresses. They wore side-hats and berets, shoes and high boots together with top coats, greatcoats and capes. Boys and girls wore certain uniforms that were based on the clothing worn by the adults.

However, upon these basic garments was built a vast complex of uniform styles, in a whole range of colours used for a multitude of purposes and worn by legions of people divided into myriads of ranks and appointments.

Colour had an important place in the subject of German uniforms, not only as uniform colour but also used as facings to greatcoat lapels, coloured tops to SA and other kepis, broad stripes and piping to trousers and breeches and as a base for insignia of rank, the latter usually indicating the wearers' branch of service or department. Certain uniform colours were used out of necessity, such as field-grey for the Army and Waffen-SS uniforms and white for Traffic Police. Other colours were chosen because they reflected the type of work undertaken by the wearer, thus black for Coal Miners, earth brown for RAD personnel, forest green for Forestry Officials etc . . . Some colours were an arbitrary choice, such as the RLB and certain municipal transport companies. Certain colours were chosen in order not to be confused with any other existing formation, thus brown was used for the uniforms of the Nazi Party, the SA and its affiliated formations. Black was chosen for the Allgemeine-SS as a colour which set them apart from all others. Eventually a black uniform became synonymous with terror and persecu-

8

tion. Some uniforms had historically been the colour they were such as the Navy with its dark navy-blue, the Luftwaffe with its adopted blue-grey similar to that worn by the RAF from which it drew its inspiration.

Despite the complexities of the various systems of ranks, appointments and levels of responsibility, the Germans adopted a method of indicating these on the uniform which was fairly consistent. The most important of these was the use of collar patches and shoulder straps. Gold or gilt insignia and buttons always took precedence over the same items in silver or white metal. In many cases cap cords or chin straps indicated degrees of responsibility. Some formations such as the NSDAP Political Leaders and the Organisation Todt adopted complex systems of arm bands designed to differentiate between the appointment levels of their members.

Indeed the Germans made full use of arm bands to indicate not only membership of a particular organisation, but also the function undertaken within that organisation as well as levels of responsibility.

Cuff-titles, which were very much a German feature of military uniforms, were used to indicate membership of particular units, participation in military campaigns or for service during past periods of historically important German history as well as being used as a form of campaign award.

Recognition for the individual who had successfully passed through a course of instruction or who was proficient in a particular trade or skill was also indicated by the wearing on the uniform of cloth or metal badges and other forms of insignia. On the uniforms worn by members of the NSDAP and all its branches distinction was made between those persons who had been members before 30 January 1933 – the date when the Nazis came to power – and those individuals who had joined after that date.

One cannot help but wonder as to the effect on the German war effort and the ultimate outcome of the war if the German nation had not worn such a profusion of uniforms and badges. If for instance they had taken to wearing blue denim suits in much the same way as did the Chinese peoples during the 1950s; doubtless it would have done nothing for their morale and esprit de corps, but it would certainly have made life much simpler for all concerned. The saving in resources in labour and material, in time spent on planning, administration, distribution and supply would have been considerable.

Great care and attention to detail has been taken with the colour art work. All the figures depicted here have been taken from contemporary black and white photographs. The colouring of the uniforms shown, and in some cases the detailing of some of the insignia, has been arrived at after painstaking research. However, because these figures are based on surviving contemporary photographs it became apparent that in a number of instances individuals had been photographed wearing items of apparel or badges and insignia to which they were not strictly entitled, whilst others were found not to be wearing these things when they should have been. Rather than attempt to correct these anomalies both Pierre Turner and I decided that we would show these figures just as they appeared. The author would be delighted to hear from anyone who may recognise himself or herself depicted in the colour plates.

The date that is shown at the heading of each section of text explaining the colour plate should only be taken as an indication as to the date the figure depicted was known to have worn that particular uniform. It does not indicate the date of introduction of the uniform, nor its withdrawal, if any.

Although by my definition there are at least ninety-four different uniformed organisations or distinct sub-units of these organisations included in this book within the 240 colour art work figures, I have had to leave out many organisations that existed during the time of the Third Reich due to lack of space.

Books of reference are seldom written in isolation and mine is no exception. I am indebted to the following persons and archives for their unstinting assistance in making available to me reference material from their own private libraries or collections or for answering questions and carrying out valuable translation work.

Individuals: Tony Froom of Rainham, Kent,; Ken Green of Fulham, London; James H. Joslyn of East Dulwich, London; James Lucas of Bromley, Kent; Andrew Mollo of Banbury, Oxfordshire; Derek and Stuart Neville of 'De Tillens', Limpsfield, Surrey; Hans Joachim Nietsche of Rattingen, West Germany; René Smeet of Brussels, Belgium; Hans D. Teske of Bletchley, Buckinghamshire; Karl Heinz (Jack) Wahnig of Euston, London; Herbert Walther of Oberlahnstein, West Germany; Jan Winters of Rotterdam, Netherlands; Miss Tracey Lazard of Blindley Heath, Surrey.

Institutions: Monty Berman, Robert (Bob) Worth and George Bennett of Messrs Bermans and Nathans, Military and Theatrical Costumiers of London who kindly allowed me the opportunity to examine items of German clothing in their collection of original garments. The Director and staff of the Imperial War Museum, London, in particular the staffs of the Photographic Library and the Printed Book Department and many other people too numerous to list individually but to whom I am greatly indebted.

The Political Leadership Hierarchy and The National Socialist German Workers Party—NSDAP

The Reichsleiter

The highest body of the Party was formed by the Reichsleitern, most of whom held at the same time leading State positions. Seventeen Ministers or Reichsleitern held office, their function included, amongst others, the following:

Police and Ministry of the Interior,
Propaganda,
Ministry of Armaments and War Production,
The Press,
Finance,
Justice,
State Labour Service,
Education of Youth,
Agriculture.

Each Reichsleiter was responsible to Hitler as President, Chancellor and Leader of the Nazi Party.

Beneath the Reichsleitung the Party was organised into Gaue, Kreise, Ortsgruppen, Zellen and Blöcke.

———

The structure of the National Socialist Party was based on forty-two Gaue (Regions) which included thirty-two in

Germany proper and ten in the annexed and occupied territories. An additional Gau – the 43rd – was created to encompass those German nationals living abroad in foreign countries. This was known as the Auslandsorganization (AO).

The Gauleiter

The Gau or Region was the original basic unit of the Nazi Party's geographical organisation as well as the largest unit in the local organisation of the Party membership.

Each Gau was headed by a Gauleiter who was appointed by, and if the need arose was removed, by Hitler. The Gau was created in the early years of the Party's history and corresponded roughly in extent with the Reichstag (German Parliament) electoral districts. It had therefore a traditional as well as a functional importance. This functional importance had been increased by war-time legislation which first gave the Gauleiter the responsibility (under the Central Government) for all matters concerning the mobilisation of labour and subsequently nominated Gaue as civil defence regions, over which the Gauleiter wielded a wide and varied authority (see the section on the National Militia – the Volkssturm).

Apart from these powers, the Gauleiter was a high-ranking Party official who was usually also the Reichsstatthalter for a Land, and moreover controlled the Gau-Wirtschaftskammer (Economic Chamber) which co-ordinated and supervised every form of trade and industry in the Gau. These additional responsibilities, entrusted to the Gauleiter by legislation, greatly increased the power of the Party and marked a distinct step in the gradual displacement by the Party Gaue of the traditional Länder or administrative regions.

Affiliated formations and organisations such as the SA, the SS, the Hitler Youth movement etc. had their main regional offices at Gau level and acted in close concert with the Gauleiter's office.

Each of the forty-two Gauleiters worked under the direction of ten Landesinspekteure, nine in Germany and one in Austria. Each inspector was charged with the responsibility for carrying out Party policy within the Gaue under his direction and with supervising the work of the Party representatives in State and Provincial legislatures. These officials controlled by the central officers of the Reichsinspection constituted the liaison between the Reichsleitung and the Gaue.

The Kreisleiter

Each Gau was divided into a number of Kreise or 'Circles', each headed by a Kreisleiter. The Kreisleiter was the lowest of the paid officials of the Party. He was directly responsible to his Gauleiter and who, on the recommendation of the Gauleiter, was nominated to this post by Hitler. The Kreisleiter's office was independent of the administrative machine and he had no direct control over the Landrat (Prefect or Head of a Distict) or the Oberbürgermeister of the very large town or the Bürgermeister of the smaller towns, although his influence was considerable.

The Ortsgruppenleiter

Beneath the Kreisleiter was the unpaid Ortsgruppenleiter or Local Group Leader appointed to the position by the Gauleiter on the nomination of the Kreisleiter.

Each Kreis consisted of a varying number of Ortsgruppen. The Ortsgruppenleiter had control over an Ortsgruppe with a population averaging approximately 40,000 and whose territory comprised one or several Communes or, in a town, a certain district. The Ortsgruppenleiter had an office of his own and controlled up to 3,000 Party members and the organization was designed to be small enough so that he could be personally acquainted with all the members.

Most of the affiliated organisations already referred to had their lowest level representation in the Ortsgruppe and often had their local office in the Ortsgruppenleiter's headquarters. They were expected to co-operate with the Ortsgruppenleiter who, however, had no disciplinary jurisdiction over them.

The Ortsgruppen were the smallest units in the rural areas but were sub-divided in a large metropolitan centre into Street Cells and Blocks (Zellen und Blöcke).

The Zellenleiter and Blockleiter

The Zellenleiter and the Blockleiter were Party officials of the lowest rank. The latter was responsible for forty to sixty households, whether or not they contained Party members; the former controlled four or five Blöcke with the assistance of Social Welfare (NS-Volkswohlfahrt -NSV) and Labour Front (Deutsche Arbeitsfront -DAF) officials.

People living in the area controlled by a Zellenleiter were encouraged to consult him, rather than higher Party officials, on any personal or technical problems. The Blockleiter was appointed to keep an eye upon the activities and political attitudes of the families under his control and to keep a card index system, containing Haushaltskarten, providing detailed information about them. Regular reports were sent from the Blockleiter to the Zellenleiter who in turn reported to his Ortsgruppenleiter and so on up through the chain of political leadership. Any unrest was dealt with swiftly and at source. Small wonder therefore that the Party found it necessary to state on repeated occasions that the Blockleiter was not employed as a Party spy.

An accurate assessment of the total membership of the NSDAP is almost impossible. By December 1943 the Party claimed that their membership included some 6,500,000 male members and 85,800 full-time officials; however a reasonable estimate of the numbers of members towards the last year of the war would have been more in the region of 7,000,000. It should not be forgotten that whilst membership of the National Socialist Party was not compulsory for the average German there were considerable advantages to be enjoyed by being a Party member. For those Germans who sought advancement in public or professional fields, Party membership was a necessary qualification for all higher governmental and professional appointments.

The Führer

1. Chancellor
   & National Leader

2. Supreme Commander

3. Party Leader

NSDAP Political Leaders

4. Regulating Leader

5. Deputy Party Leader

6. Political Assistant

7. District
   & Group Leader

8. Party Standard Bearer

9. Senior Regulating Leader

NSDAP Political Leaders

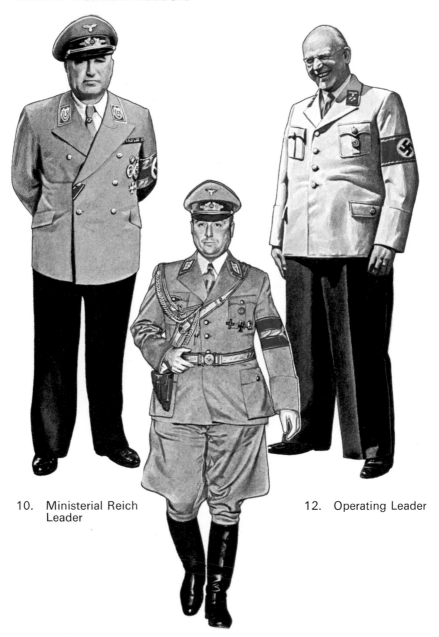

10. Ministerial Reich
    Leader

11. Regional Leader

12. Operating Leader

13. Leadership School
Adjutant

15. Senior Coordinating
Leader

14. Drum Major

Storm Troops

16. SA Soldier

17. SA Chief of Staff

18. SA Musician

19. SA Police Officer

20. SA Police Officer

21. SA Staff Guard

Storm Troops

22. Leadership School
    Staff Officer

23. SA Chief of Staff

24. SA Officer

25. SA Officer

26. SA Honour Guard

27. SA Sportsman

Storm Troops & Naval Storm Troops

28. Marine SA Man

30. Marine SA Officer

29. SA Storm Leader

31. Motor School Instructor

33. NSKK Dispatch Rider

32. NSKK Officer

National Socialist Motorised Corps

34. NSKK Guard

35. NSKK Traffic Policeman

36. NSKK Officer

Stahlhelm & Brigade Ehrhardt Veteran Soldiers Units

37. Brigade Ehrhardt NCO

39. Stahlhelm Standard
     Bearer

38. Stahlhelm Officer

The General-SS

40. SS Sentry

41. Reichsleader SS

42. Protection Squad Man

43. SS Adjutant

45. SS Officer

44. Security Service Chief

The General-SS

46. SS Mess Waiter

47. Elite Honour Guard

48. SS Guard Officer

49. SS-VT Recruit

50. SS-VT Officer Instructor

51. SS-VT Officer

The Hitler Youth

52. Reich Youth Leader

53. Youth

54. HJ Officer

55. HJ Anti-Aircraft
     Auxiliary

56. Auxiliary Fire
     Service Youth

57. Special Patrol
     Service Youth

The Hitler Youth – Naval Branch

58. Marine Youth

60. Marine Youth

59. Marine Youth Officer

61. Land Service Girl

62. BDM National
Departmental Leader

63. BDM Girl

The Hitler Youth – Junior Section (Boys)

64. DJ 'Pimpf'

65. DJ Drum Major

66. DJ File Leader

67. FAD Musician

69. Labour Service Volunteer

68. FAD Officer

National Labour Service

70. National Labour
    Service Musician

71. RAD Instructor

72. RAD Officer

73. Labour Service Guard

74. Reich Labour Leader

75. RAD Medical Officer

National Labour Service – Women's Section

76. Agricultural Worker

77. RADwJ Official

78. RADwJ District Officer

79. DAF Works NCO

81. Labour Front Musician

80. DAF Political Official

National Socialist Flying Corps.

82. NSFK Man

83. NSFK Colonel

84. NSFK Standard Bearer

85. NPEA Student

86. NPEA Officer Instructor

87. NPEA Honour Guard

German Army

88. Field Marshal

89. Lieutenant-General

90. Guard Captain

91. Field Marshal

92. High Command Official

93. Tank Corporal

German Army

94. Administrative Official

96. Cavalry NCO

95. Field Bishop

German Army

97. Senior Corporal

98. Grenadier

99. Supply Driver

German Army

100. Field Policeman

101. SP Artillery NCO

102. Field Police NCO

103. Infantry Sniper

105. Mountain Troop Officer

104. Infantry NCO

German Army Female Auxiliaries

106. Army Signals Auxiliary

108. Army Signals Auxiliary

107. Signals Auxiliary Officer

109. Grand Admiral

110. Drum Major

111. Captain

German Navy

112. Mate

113. Lieutenant

114. Seaman 1st Class

115. Submariner

116. Adminstrative Official

117. Seaman

German Navy & Female Auxiliaries

118. U-Boat Commander

119. Captain

120. Female Naval Assistant

121. Marine Artillery
Adjutant

123. Marine Artillery
General

122. Marine Artillery Seaman

German Air Sports Organisation

124. DLV Officer

125. Air Traffic Supervisory NCO

126. DLV Airman

127.   Reich Marshal

129.   Reich Marshal

128.   Reich Marshal

German Air Force

130. Signals Lieutenant

131. Colonel-General

132. Administrative General

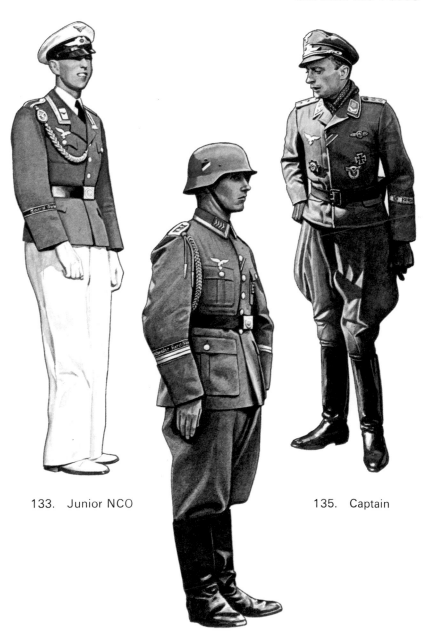

133. Junior NCO

135. Captain

134. Staff NCO

German Air Force

136. Fighter Pilot

137. Airman

138. Flight NCO—
Bombers

139. Tank Crew Lieutenant

141. Engineer Corps General

140. Legion Condor
Captain

142. Captain

143. Paratrooper

144. Paratroop Field Policeman

145. HG Division
Soldier

146. Paratroop Division Major

147. Field Division Soldier

German Air Force & SS Female Auxiliaries

148. Anti-Aircraft Auxiliary

150. Air Force Signals
Auxiliary

149. SS Auxiliary

151. SS Brigade Leader
     & Major General

153. SS Musician

152. SS Lieutenant

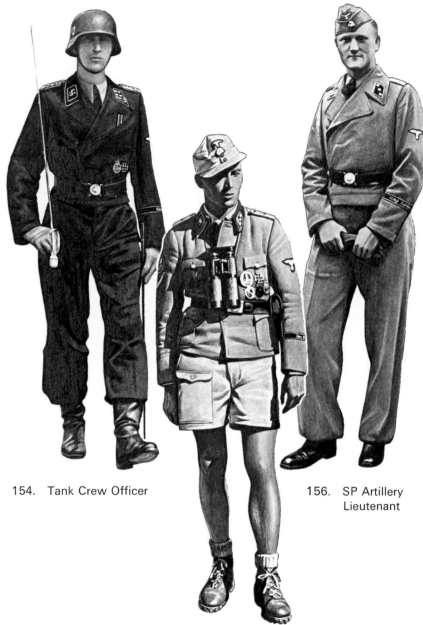

154. Tank Crew Officer

155. Lieutenant

156. SP Artillery
      Lieutenant

157.   SS Corporal

158.   SS Senior Private

159.   SS Staff Sergeant

Armed-SS

160. SS Sergeant

162. SS Private

161. SS Staff Sergeant

163. Traffic Control
     NCO

164. Municipal Police Officer

165. Municipal Police Musician

German Police Formations

166. Autobahn Police Officer

167. Coastal Police Officer

168. Rural Police NCO

169. Mountain Police Junior NCO

171. Fire Police NCO

170. General of Uniformed Police

German Police Formations

172. Waterways Police
     Lieutenant

174. Combat Police
     Regimental Officer

173. Customs Governmental
     Councillor

175. Railway Protection
Policeman

177. Barrack Police Trooper

176. Order Police Lieutenant-General

German Police Formations

178. Motorized Traffic
Policeman

179. Administrative Police Officer

180. Police Tank Crew
NCO

181. Landpolice NCO

182. Prison Service Official

183. Female Police
      Auxiliary

German Peoples Army

184. Party Member Volunteer

185. Brigade Medical Officer

186. Volunteer Youth

187.   Foreign Minister

188.   German Ambassador

189.   Foreign Minister

Diplomatic & Government Officials

190.   Diplomatic Official

192.   Diplomatic Official

191.   Government Minister

193. Territorial
     Assistant

195. Construction Unit
     Officer

194. Ministerial Director

Air Defence League

196. RLB Lieutenant

197. President

198. RLB Attendant

Security & Rescue Service/Air Raid Warning Service

199.   SHD Man

200.   SHD Unit Leader

201.   LSW Unit Leader

Factory Guards

202. Factory Guard Officer

203. Factory Guard NCO

204. Factory Guard NCO

205. DRK Head Nursing
Sister

206. DRK Officer

207. DRK Man

German Red Cross

208. DRK Nurse

209. Senior Red Cross General

210. DRK Nurse

211. Senior Overseer

213. Construction Worker

212. Minister of Armanents
& War Production

Emergency, Construction & Transport Units

214. Resque Squad Man

215. OT General

216. Transport Legion Officer

217. TeNo Troop Leader

219. TeNo Foreman

218. Emergency Unit Commander

Forestry & Falconry Officials

220. Senior Hunting
Master

222. National Hunting Master

221. District Falconry Master

223. NSKOV Official

225. Colonial League Officer

224. NS-RKB Official

German State Railways

226. Central Office
     Secretary

227. Communications Official

228. Senior Locomotive
     Driver

**German
State Railways**

229. Survey Inspector

230. Auxiliary Worker

231. Railway Assistant

German Postal Service

232. Postal Works Assistant

233. Postal Protection NCO

234. Auxiliary Postal
Driver

235.
Tram Conductress

237. Bus Conductor

236. BDM Auxiliary Postal Worker

German Coal Miners

238.   Mining Overseer

239.   Mining Official

240.   Apprentice Miner

Plate Descriptions

1,2,3.
The Führer, Adolf Hitler: 1) Der Führer und Reichs-kanzler, 1937, Political Uniform. 2) Oberster Befehls-haber der Deutschen Wehrmacht, 1942, Military Uniform. 3) Der Führer, 9 November 1934, Political Brown Shirt Uniform.

The three most important uniforms worn by Adolf Hitler are shown here. In the early days of the Nazi Movement Hitler more often than not would wear civilian clothing over which he habitually wore a somewhat crumpled and sometimes grubby belted raincoat, occasionally topped off with a soft, wide-brimmed felt hat. At those events when he addressed gatherings or reviewed parades of his Party followers he invariably wore the style of Brown Shirt uniform in use at that time. Later when he had established himself as the undisputed leader of the German nation as well as of the Nazi Party for special commemorative events he occasionally wore a refined version of the original Brown Shirt uniform (Fig. 3). There is only one recorded instance of when Hitler actually wore the SA kepi (which as will be explained was also worn during the Movement's formative years by Political Leaders of the NSDAP as well as by members of the SA, see (Fig. 7)). A portrait photograph taken of Hitler by his personal photographer Heinrich Hoffmann showed him wearing the SA kepi. Hitler so disliked the image he saw that not only was the photograph never released but Hitler never wore any form of headdress with his Brown Shirt uniform. The so-called 'Political Uniform' (Fig. 1) was devised in order that Hitler could wear a form of military style uniform more in keeping with his rôle as National Leader and Chancellor of the German People. When England declared war on Germany on 3 September 1939 Hitler took to wearing a field-grey uniform that reflected his wartime rôle as Supreme Commander of the German Armed Forces. In

97

place of the Nazi Party swastika arm band he wore a gold version of the Armed Forces National Emblem (Fig. 2).

In a nation whose people had a love of, and a reverence for, uniformed attire Adolf Hitler was unique. He ranked above all others, sometimes holding a military position or a para-military cum political appointment without equal. Other times he administered from a position far removed from and above even the most senior persons all of whom were actually categorised by terms of rank. Because of his unique status Hitler wore uniforms that did not actually represent any one organisation and which were of a simple design worn without elaboration, without trimmings, without marks of rank and always with just a few military and political awards and badges. Those badges and awards he wore with obvious pride were those that he had deservedly earned during the First World War and during the 'Period of Struggle' of the Movement. These were: The Imperial German Iron Cross, 1st Class awarded on 4 August 1918, the Imperial German Wound Badge in black awarded on 18 May 1918 – Hitler having been wounded in the left thigh on 5 October 1916 and gassed during the last weeks of the war. The Golden Honour Badge of the Party, worn above the Iron Cross and the Black Wound Badge marked the fact, as it did for the other recipients, that he had been amongst the first 100,000 members of the National Socialist German Workers Party.

4.
NSDAP Political Leader: Stellenleiter in Kreisleitung, 1937.

The Political Leaders uniform evolved like the uniforms of other organisations and the introduction of the four pocket jacket as shown here came after the shirt and breeches style uniform (see Figures 5, 7).

Rank insignia of all periods was habitually worn on the collar. Political leaders, with the notable exception of the very first style of uniform (Figs 5 & 7) and the Political Leadership Training School officials (Fig. 13), did not wear shoulder straps. In the early days of the Movement one of the number of different ways devised to distinguish individual ranks and group responsibility was by the use of collar patches of varying designs combined with set combinations of colours. Plain swastika arm bands of the normal Party style were re-introduced without regard to the wearer's rank.

5.
NSDAP Political Leader: Deputy Party Leader (Stellvertreter), Rudolf Hess, 1934.

Rudolf Hess, one of the earliest members of the Nazi Party, who having joined in June 1920 rose in 1933 to become the Deputy Leader of the Party. He is shown here wearing an early style of Political Leaders uniform. It is noticeable that there is no insignia of rank being worn, doubtless following the style of the Führer. The cap is one of the earliest types of peaked cap with only the small early pattern political eagle and swastika emblem being worn without the cockade, as shown in Figure 4.

6.
NSDAP Political Leader: Ortsgruppenhelfer, 1943.

The uniforms for NSDAP Political Leaders underwent a number of changes and the one illustrated here, correctly referred to as Service Dress with Greatcoat, represents the final pattern of greatcoat.

By 1943 the rank and appointment insignia had undergone four complete changes (see Figs 4 and 7 for two earlier styles) before finally being developed into an elaborate and seemingly complex system of 95 different appointments and four separate areas of Political responsibility.

The insignia on the cap was the most elaborate of all the previous cap insignia and the swastika arm bands in their final form had developed into a systematic means of indicating the level of function held by the wearer within the political system.

In sharp contrast to Fig. 4 the parade harness in light Havana-brown leather was more elaborate than anything that had been previously worn, with the introduction of the cross strap worn together with supporting straps for the pack and a waist belt, the gilt buckle of which displayed the German Eagle set within a wreath of oak leaves.

7.8.9.
NSDAP Political Leaders: 7) Landesinspektor und Fraktionsführer des Reichstages, 1930, early pattern Political Leaders Service Uniform. 8) Fahnenträger der Ortsgruppen, 1940, Ceremonial Dress. 9) Haupstellenleiter bei der Ortsgruppe, 1944, Service Uniform.

The uniforms worn by Political Leaders of the National Socialist German Workers Party during the formative years of the Movement were in many ways similar in appearance to those worn by members of the Sturmabteilungen (SA). Both wore the Austrian pattern kepi, which even for the SA was originally plain brown colour. Both formations wore the Brown shirt and brown leather waist belt together with brown (and not necessarily matching) breeches and high boots. It was during these early days of the Movement – referred to by the Nazis as the 'Kampfzeit' or 'Period of Struggle' – that many items of insignia and types of uniforms were introduced, the majority of which were shortlived. An example of some of these insignia can be seen in Fig. 7. Rank was indicated for a Political Leader by the use of chin strap cords in either silver or gilt which was either plain or had one or two plaited knots. The same system applied to the series of thin shoulder straps used. The small black, diamond-shaped cloth badge bearing an early style eagle and swastika emblem was the arm badge used to indicate that the wearer was a Political Leader and originally it was worn without a swastika armband. Later both were worn together. The small strip of black cloth worn below the Political Leaders arm badge displayed the year of the wearer's date of enrolment into the Nazi Party.

The swastika arm band with the three bands of white was one of a number of such arm bands used during this early period to indicate various levels of appointment. The small black cloth badge displaying a coloured shield worn on the right forearm was used to indicate that the wearer was a 'Fraktionsführer des Reichstages', a Leader of a parliamentary faction in the German State Parliament. The 'Landesfarben' or heraldic colours used on the shield were those of the Land represented by the Political Leader, here shown as blue and white for Bavaria.

Flag Bearers of the Political Leadership Corps were distinguished by the use of a gorget referred to as a 'Brustschild für Fahnenträger', the wearing of white buckskin gauntlets and a carrying sash or baldric. The colouring of this last item was different for each of the three political levels, Orts, Kreis and Gau in that it matched the colours and piping of the flag bearers' own collar patches, as is the case here in Fig. 8.

It is beyond doubt that the bombing offensive launched against German towns and cities contributed in a very large measure to the ultimate defeat of the German nation. Although this destruction heaped upon the German people during the daytime by the US Army Air Force and at night by RAF Bomber Command in an almost continuous stream of air raids may have helped to destroy their means to fight it should be remembered that, just as with the Londoners during the Blitz, their resolve to survive and to continue the fight, if anything, was stiffened. 'Our walls may break but never our hearts' was just one of many slogans that were painted on walls throughout Germany.

The Selbstschutz (Self-Protection Service) was the organisation created for the protection of the ordinary householder based on a Warden and Fire-guard system. Each house (generally a block of flats) had a House Warden. Over him was a Blockwart (Block Warden) (see Fig. 198) who controlled several streets under the supervision of a Ward Protection Leader, thus following closely the organisation of the Nazi Party. After particularly severe air raids when the fire-fighting and rescue services were stretched to their limits every able-bodied person, and especially members of the Party's organisations, who could be made available and who lived or worked in the vicinity were expected to assist the Police and the Fire Police. They helped in rescuing trapped people, in fighting fires, recovering possessions and goods and in administering first aid. In 1942 a 'Leader' was appointed to take charge of several Self-Protection groups with the power to transfer reinforcements from one area to another under heavy raid conditions. The Landluftschutz-gemeinschaft (Rural Air Raid Protection Fellowship) pro-vided fire-fighting and rescue squads in rural areas too small to be served by any of the other service. Post-air raid service such as emergency feeding, billeting, and re-housing, the operation of rest centres and information services, and mass evacuation from high risk danger areas were organised by the Nazi Party auxiliary organisations to supplement the regular municipal services.

Although a regulation pattern steel helmet had been introduced to be worn by members of these Self-Protection units (see Fig. 199) deficiencies were often made up by issuing steel helmets captured from other armies or surplus to requirements, as is the case in Fig. 9 where a Russian steel helmet is shown being worn by a Political Leader carrying out air raid rescue work in 1944.

10.
NSDAP Political Leader: Reichsleiter Dr Robert Ley, 1943.

Ley is wearing the double breasted walking-out uniform consisting of a brown jacket, black trousers trimmed with a

25 mm. wide band of black silk, white shirt and light brown tie.

Medals, decorations, awards and ribbons were permitted to be worn on this jacket. Dr Ley is shown here wearing a medal ribbon bar on the left upper breast, below which he is wearing his Golden Party Badge in line with the Hitler Youth Golden Badge of Honour. Below these are his First World War Wound Badge together with his Imperial Observers badge and below this again he wears the Nazi War Merit Cross in silver without swords. The ribbon worn in the button hole is that of the 'Blood Order' or the 'Decoration of 9 November 1923'.

11.
NSDAP Political Leader: Gauleiter, 1944.

The Gauleiter shown here is wearing the Political Leaders full ceremonial uniform complete with gold coloured Aiguillettes, waist belt and cross strap. Suspended from the belt is the light Havana-brown leather holster containing the 'Honour Pistol'.

The Political Leaders ceremonial uniform was to have been worn on all ceremonial and official occasions involving the Party, its organisations and associated groups, the Armed Forces and the State etc., or for any function when Political Leaders appeared as guests of honour.

12.
NSDAP Political Leader: Einsatzleiter in Gauleitung. 1942.

This uniform known as Office Dress consisted of a white linen jacket worn together with dark brown trousers. No medals were allowed to be worn with this jacket although the Party membership badge or the Golden Party Badge of Honour were permitted. Rank was shown by the use of collar patches and insignia of function level was displayed on the arm band. The coloured piping to the collar patches and the arm band indicated the State group of the wearer, which in this case was red, that of Gauleitung level.

As with other buttons used on Political Leaders uniforms of this period the buttons as worn were in gilt coloured metal showing a small representation of the German National Emblem. This style of uniform was not permitted to be worn in the street unless it was worn under the greatcoat or cloak. A pistol was not to be worn with this office dress.

13.
NSDAP Political Leader: Adjutant auf dem Ordensburgen der NSDAP, 1943, Service Uniform.

Members of the staffs at all three of the Ordensburgen (Leadership Schools), Krössinsee, Sonthofen and Vogelsang wore the same style of uniform. It was very similar to the standard Political Leaders uniform but was distinguished by the use of shoulder straps worn in pairs and a brown and yellow cuff-title worn on the left cuff. This last item displayed the name of the Leadership School of which the wearer was a member of the staff. The swastika arm band bore no insignia of office but was piped in coloured piping of the level of the leadership to which the wearer already belonged. Collar patches were worn by staff members but were not worn by Political Candidates; however Fig. 13 shows an Adjutant on the staff of the Vogelsang Ordensburg not wearing collar patches.

14.
NSDAP Political Leader: Ortsgruppen Bereitschaftsleiter Spielmannszugführer, 1943, Ceremonial Dress.

Musicians in the Political Leadership Corps followed the same practice employed by other musicians of most other uniformed organisations in that they wore Musicians Wings or 'Swalbennester'-Swallows Nests on their uniforms (see also Figs 18, 38, 65, 67, 70, 81, 153 & 165). Three grades of

Musicians existed at three levels within the Party system. All the Swallows Nests were braided in flat gold braid decorated with a fine patterning of gold swastikas. For Musicians of all grades at Regional or Gau level the backing colour to the gold braiding was in bright red, at District or Kreis level it was in dark brown cloth and at Local or Ortsgruppen level it was in light brown material. Swalbennester used by Drum Majors – Spielmannszugführer – at any of the three above mentioned levels had a 5 cm. deep gold fringe to the lower edge of the nests (Fig. 14), Bandsmen or Musiker had a 3 cm. deep gold fringe and Musicians or Spielmänner had plain Swallows Nests worn without a fringe.

15.
NSDAP Political Leader: Hauptbereichsleiter in Gauleitung, 1944, Greatcoat.

When worn open at the neck the Political Leaders greatcoat revealed lapels of a light coffee colour. Compare this method with that shown in Figure 6. The use of the 'Afrika' with Palms cuff-title by a member of the Political Leadership Corps was unusual but not unknown. Normally associated with being awarded to members of the German Army or Air Force this cuff-title was classed as a campaign award. It was introduced on 15 January 1943 to replace the earlier 'Afrikakorps' cuff-title which had been intended only to have been worn by members of the Afrikakorps actually fighting in North Africa. Conditions of eligibility for the award of the 'Afrika' cuff-title were:
1) At least six months service in an operational theatre in North Africa, less if wounded, or
2) Being invalided out of the Armed Forces as a result of contracting a tropical disease after having served at least three months in an operational theatre in North Africa or
3) It was awarded to anyone, irrespective of length of service in North Africa, who had won a German decoration whilst serving in North Africa.

Another known instance of an Army cuff-title worn on an unusual uniform was that of the 'Grossdeutschland' cuff-title (silver on black version) worn by former Reichsjugendführer Baldur von Schirach on his Political Leaders uniform when he held the office of Gauleiter of Vienna.

16.
Storm Troops: Senior Troop Leader, SA Wehrmannschaft, 1943, SA Wehrmannschafts Uniform.

With the coming of the Second World War the SA was put on a war footing. Vast numbers of its members were drafted into the Armed Forces and by 1945 as much as 80 per cent of its pre-war membership of three million men was serving in the armed forces. By a decree of 1939 Hitler created the SA Wehrmannschaften or SA Military Training Defence Groups. These Groups were entrusted with military training both preceding and following the period of regular military service. It was also made responsible for training those males unfit to be accepted by the Armed Forces. The Wehrmannschaften together with other war activities helped restore to the depleted SA some of its lost importance. The demands of the war also gave prominence to the special SA formations listed below.

The ordinary rank and file and junior officers of the SA Wehrmannschaften were distinguished from the regular SA by the use of a specially designed Service Cap, modelled it would seem on the similar cap worn by Italian Army troops. Cuff-titles were worn which carried the name of an individual Wehrmannschaft unit and in 1939 the shoulder straps, originally used by the SA for the lower ranks of its formations, underwent a complete revision. The multitude of different straps with their coloured underlays used to indicate various SA districts were abolished. In their place new shoulder straps were introduced worn in pairs which reflected the rôle in which the SA now found itself. All straps had light brown braiding with a fine silver-white chevron design but the nine basic colours used as underlays indicated the following formations: Carmine red: Senior SA Officers, Bright red: SA Group Staff, Light Grey: Foot Units including SA Standarte 'Feldherrnhalle', Emerald Green: Jäger (light infantry), Rifle and Mountain troop units, Lemon Yellow: Signals troops, Gold Yellow: SA Cavalry, Dark Blue: Marine SA Detachments, Mid-Blue: SA Medical units, Black: SA Engineer units.

17.
Storm Troops: Stabschef der SA Ernst Röhm, 1933, SA Officers Uniform.

Born in 1887 Ernst Röhm had been a professional soldier for most of his early adult life. As an Army Captain he had been a Company Commander in the 10th Bavarian Infantry Regiment and after the war he had served as political adviser on the staff of General Ritter von Epp, whose Freikorps had 'liberated' Munich from the Communists in 1919. He became a member of the Nazi Party almost from the start and during those early days of the Movement it was he who helped Hitler to organise the fledgling Hall-Guards, later to become known as the Storm Detachments (Sturmabteilung, SA). He left the German Army in 1923 and devoted all his time to building up the SA, the leadership of which was first held by Johann Ulrich Klintsch and then by Hermann Göring. He took part in the Munich Putsch of November 1923 and with its failure was arrested and imprisoned. On his release, and with Hitler still in Landsberg prison, it was Röhm and Alfred Rosenberg who kept alive the banned Nazi Movement. When Hitler was released from prison he reformed the National Socialist Party and Röhm was once more placed in charge of re-organising and expanding the

SA. But disagreement between Röhm and Hitler as to the future course that the SA should take set in which resulted in Röhm leaving Germany in May 1925 to serve as a Staff Officer in the Bolivian Army. During his absence and with Göring in exile and from the time it had been reformed in November 1926 the leadership of the SA was taken on by Captain Franz Felix Pfeffer von Salomon.

Five years later in October 1930 Röhm was recalled to Germany by Hitler and with the dismissal of von Salomon, Röhm was appointed Chief-of-Staff of the SA. Hitler took upon himself the position of Supreme Leader of the SA (Oberster SA Führer OSAF). Röhm retained this position up to the time of his murder by order of Hitler as part of the massive purge that was inflicted on the SA Leadership on the night of 30 June 1934.

Ernst Röhm is shown here (Fig. 17) in the SA Tunic and breeches introduced into the SA after June 1932. The use of coloured collar patches and coloured tops to the SA Officers kepi had been in use since August 1929. The collar patch emblem of a gilt six-pointed star set within a wreath of laurel leaves was in all probability designed by Röhm himself or at least on his insistence as the star emblem was copied from those worn by Generals of the Bolivian Army.

18.
Storm Troops: SA-Truppführer and Musician from the Horst Wessel Detachment, Berlin-Brandenburg SA District, 1933. The 'Tradition Uniform'.

The brown shirt worn together with brown breeches, high boots and kepi as shown here in Fig. 18 was the uniform that had evolved over the years from the first beginings when only a swastika arm band existed to distinguish the members of the early Hall-Guards. Although the uniform as shown in Figs 17, 24 and 25 became after 1933 the standard type of uniform worn by SA Officers the brown shirt outfit was occasionally worn after this date as a 'Tradition Uniform'.

19,20.

Storm Troops: 19) Obertruppführer, SA Auxiliary Police Berlin-Brandenburg, 1933, Greatcoat as Winter Service Dress. 20) FJK-Sturmführer, Feldjägerkorps, 1934, Ceremonial Dress.

In an effort to increase and maintain strict standards of discipline and correct behaviour within the growing, and somewhat undisciplined, ranks of the SA, a special unit of handpicked men chosen from amongst the SA, the SS and the Stahlhelm was formed, charged with the task of acting as an internal police force. Originally this unit, which was formed on 22 February 1933 at the instigation of Hermann Göring, Commander-in-Chief of the Prussian Police, was known as the 'SA Auxiliary Police of the Group Berlin-Brandenburg' (Hilfspolizei der Gruppe Berlin-Brandenburg). In March of that same year it was retitled 'Field Police of the Group Berlin-Brandenburg' (Feldpolizei der Gruppe Berlin-Brandenburg. The units strength consisted of three Bereitschaften or readiness squads each of sixty men. The men of these squads wore SA uniform and kepi but with a police greatcoat of blue cloth. Their distinctive insignia consisted of a 'Police Star' mounted on to the right hand, black collar patch – the left hand patch showed the wearer's rank – and these patches were worn on both their tunics and greatcoats. The white metal 'Police Star' insignia was also worn on the front of their black topped SA kepi (black was used as the district colour for the Berlin-Brandenburg SA units). When on duty these SA Police wore a white metal duty gorget (Fig. 19).

On 1 October 1933 Göring raised a new unit to be known as the 'Feldjägerkorps in Prussia'. Most of the men from the former Field Police units were transferred to this new formation and additional manpower was selected from amongst officers and men of the SA, SS and the SA-Reserve. This new formation had increased powers of discipline. Himmler gave orders that it was to be regarded as a special unit outside the normal area of the established SA and SS units and its regulations laid down that when on duty any members of the Feldjägerkorps were considered to be superior to all SA and SS officers and men. Their uniform was changed to a white-piped olive-brown tunic and olive-brown breeches worn with brown leather waist belt and cross strap. They wore white collar patches bearing a gilt metal 'Police Star' (right side) and gilt rank insignia (left side) with white tops to their SA kepis. As a mark of office they wore a white metal duty gorget (Ringkragen) which indicated their FJK unit number and they carried long bladed police bayonets.

This new formation under the direct control of SA Chief-of-Staff Ernst Röhm (Fig. 17) and commanded by Oberführer Fritsch consisted of eight detachments or 'Feldjäger-Abteilungen' each of three Feldjägerbereitschaften with 65 men to each squad. These were numbered and stationed as follows: I Königsberg, II Stettin, IIIa Breslau, IIIb Berlin, IV Magdeburg, V Frankfurt am Main, VIa Hannover and VIb Düsseldorf. On 1 April 1935 these units were incorporated into the Reich Protection Police and ceased from that time to have direct Party association (see Fig. 166).

21.
Storm Troops: SA-Truppführer, Stabswache Göring, 1934, Greatcoat as Parade Dress.

When Ernst Röhm was appointed Chief-of-Staff of the SA in January 1931 he set up a number of 'Stabswachen' or Staff Guards, sometimes referred to as Headquarters Guards. These guards were formed to provide a reliable bodyguard of armed officers and men of at least one year's service in the SA or SS who were made responsible for the protection of an individual and his staff considered of importance to the

National Socialist Movement. A Staff Guard was set up to protect the Supreme SA Leader (Stabswache der Obersten SA-Führung), which at that time was Ernst Röhm. Hermann Göring was provided with a Staff Guard known as 'Stabswache Göring' (Fig. 21) and Staff Guards were organised for SA Leaders of Groups and Senior Groups 'Stabswachen der Obergruppen und Gruppen'. Adolf Hitler had an entire regiment as his bodyguard known as 'Standarte Adolf Hitler'. The members of the Hermann Göring Staff Guard wore bright red cuff-titles bearing the inscription in silver lettering 'Stabswache Göring'. They wore the normal pattern SA uniforms – both tunics and the brown shirt – together with greatcoats and brown coloured steel helmets. Because these bodyguards were armed they came to be considered as part of the threat to Hitler and the Nazi Movement represented by Röhm with his ambition to create a 'brown army' from 'his' stormtroopers. With the murder of Röhm and the purge of many of the leading SA Officers these Staff Guards were disbanded – all that is except the SA-Standarte 'Adolf Hitler', which developed into the SS-Leibstandarte Adolf Hitler (LSAH).

22,23,24.
Storm Troops: 22) SA-Obersturmbannführer, 1944, SA Military Training Service Uniform. 23) SA-Stabschef Viktor Lutze, 1941, White Summer Tunic as Full Dress. 24) SA-Sturmbannführer, 1940, Service Uniform.

The SA Tunic referred to as the 'SA-Wehrmannschafts-Dienstrock' and designed to be worn closed at the neck was introduced for use during the war years. It was not a common item and photographic evidence shows it to have been worn only by officers. Members of the Staff of the SA Leadership School situated at Munich (SA-Reichs-Führerschule) wore red collar patches which had the black and white Tyr-rune on the right hand patch and their rank insignia on the left hand patch (Fig. 22). Pupils at this same school wore the Tyr-rune on both patches. Those persons who had sucessfully passed through the Munich leadership school to become officers in the SA were permitted to wear on the left upper arm of their SA uniforms the same Tyr-rune emblem (Fig. 22, 23).

Viktor Lutze took over the position of SA Chief-of-Staff shortly after Röhm had been eliminated. Lutze was born at Bevergern, Westphalia, on 28 December 1890. During the 1914–18 war he had served in Infantry Regiment 369 and Reserve Infantry Regiment 15. He joined the Nazi Party in 1922. He was appointed by Hitler to be Police President of Hanover in February 1933 and in March 1934 he was made Prefect of Hanover. Lutze was killed along with his daughter in what was officially described as a 'motoring accident' during the summer of 1943 and his place was taken by the final SA Chief-of-Staff Wilhelm Scheppmann.

The white Summer Tunic could be worn as Undress Uniform or, when worn with the 'SA-Feldbinde' the SA officers brocade waist belt, the tunic became Full Dress wear for summer use. The Honour Dagger of the German Army being worn by Lutze in Fig. 23 was unique within the diverse miscellany of daggers worn by officers of all the varied uniformed organisations. It was presented to SA Chief-of-Staff Viktor Lutze on 28 December 1940 on the occasion of his fiftieth birthday by General Field Marshal von Brauchitsch on behalf of the German Army. For many years after the Second World War this dagger was the centre piece of a very fine collection of German daggers and edged weapons belonging to an English collector.

During the war the SA-Dienstrock or Service Tunic (Fig. 24) underwent a slight modification. The side pockets to the tunic 'skirt' were produced with pleats and most noticeably, with the simplification of the colouring system used for the collar patches and shoulder straps (see text to Fig. 16), the shoulder straps were worn in pairs.

112

25.
Storm Troops: SA-Obertruppführer, 1934, Evening Dress.

The SA did not provide its members with a Dress Uniform for formal or informal evening wear in the same way as did the Luftwaffe (Fig. 130). However the SA did possess a form of evening wear. It consisted of the standard four pocket SA tunic worn together with red piped, black trousers, a white shirt and brown tie. Medals were worn on the tunic but no headdress was worn with this attire.

26.
Storm Troops: SA-Oberscharführer, SA-Standarte 'Feldherrnhalle', 1936, Greatcoat as Guard Uniform.

Viktor Lutze was appointed SA Chief-of-Staff in July 1934. One of the first acts he undertook was to raise a special SA unit composed of handpicked volunteers. This elite SA Regiment consisted of six battalions housed in barracks and stationed throughout Germany at Berlin, Munich, Hattingen, Krefeld, Stettin and Stuttgart. This new formation had the distinction of bearing arms and service in the Regiment counted as military service. The Regiment received its title of SA-Standarte 'Feldherrnhalle' from Hitler during the Nuremberg Party rally of September 1936. Members of the Regiment were distinguished by wearing a light brown cuff-title bearing the silver wording 'Feldherrnhalle' on their left sleeve. All ranks up to and including SA-Obersturmbannführer displayed the Regimental emblem (Wolfsengel) on their carmine red coloured collar patches (right side only). When on duty all ranks wore a special metal gorget (Fig. 26).

27.
Storm Troops: SA-Mann, 1940, Sports Clothing.

This figure, the only one of its kind in this book, has been included in order to represent the sports clothing as used by many of the military and para-military formations in Germany during the Third Reich period. Sports clothing as such can be divided into three categories; a) Track Suits, b) Sports Kit for field events and ball games and c) Swimming Suits used for water sports.

Most organisations used much the same design for their sports clothing. Only the colour of the articles varied from one organisation to another as did the emblems they carried sewn on to the sports vests, shorts or track suits. The German Air Force had the most elaborate system in that they actually indicated grades of proficiency at swimming by the use of different coloured swimming trunks as well as markings on their sports vests to indicate military rank.

The SA emblem was displayed on the front of the sports vest in the colour of the wearer's SA district colour (Fig. 27). The emblem also incorporated, in small lettering, the abbreviated form of the name of that same SA district.

28, 29, 30.
Storm Troops and Naval Storm Troops: 28) SA-Marine Oberscharführer, 1935, Service Uniform. 29) SA-Sturmführer, 1938, Special Service Uniform. 30) SA-Marine Sturmführer, SA-Marine Service Dress.

A naval (Marine) section of the SA had existed from as early as 1933. As a branch of the SA it was intended to bring together all those members who were sailors by profession, deep sea, coastal waters and inland waterways or who had served in the Reichsmarine during the 1914–18 war. Their peace-time function was two-fold. To act as a form of naval ambassador for the German people in being representatives of the new National Socialist Movement when coming into contact with seamen from other maritime nations, and to be available to assist in cases of disaster concerning waterborne craft. Towards these ends the members of the Marine-SA were trained professionally in seamanship and were indoctrinated politically. During the war, those members of the Marine-SA that were not drafted into the Kriegsmarine were used as instructors to teach members of the Marine-HJ the art of seamanship in preparation for their joining the regular war-time navy.

Members of Marine-SA units wore uniforms of navy blue material and with practically all their metal insignia, buttons, some braiding and metal fittings in gilt. Fig. 28 shows the first pattern Marine-SA uniform, similar in general appearance to the SA Brown Shirt uniform of the same period, except of course for the basic colour and the use of a peaked cap in place of the SA kepi. Fig. 30 shows the uniform introduced for all ranks of the Marine-SA after 1934.

Members of SA units from the SA districts of 'Hochland' (Fig. 29), 'Alpenland', 'Donau' and 'Südmark' were permitted to wear the traditional German Lederhosen or leather shorts as part of their summer uniform. This privilege applied to Political Leaders from these same areas. It is recorded that Reichsführer-SS Himmler had entertained the idea of attiring guard units of his men from those SS districts in the south of Germany also in Lederhosen.

31, 32, 33, 34, 35, 36.
National Socialist Motorised Corps: 31) NSKK-Obersturmführer, Technical Leaders School Instructor, 1940, Service Uniform. 32) NSKK-Obersturmführer, NSKK-Detachment 'Ernst von Rath', 1939, Traditional Brown Shirt Uniform. 33) NSKK-Oberscharführer, Stabe der Motorobergruppe 'Ost', 1942, Protective Motoring Suit. 34) NSKK-Obersturmmann, 1943, Guard Uniform. 35) NSKK-Truppführer, 1939, Service Uniform. 36) NSKK-Sturmführer, 1935, Winter Full Dress Uniform.

The origins of the NSKK (Nationalsozialistischen Kraftfahrkorps) can be found in two distinct motor vehicle organisations; the Nationalsozialistischen Automobil Korps (NSAK) and the Motor-SA (MSA).

The NSAK was founded on 1 April 1930 and as part of the SA its first leader was the Supreme SA Leader Hauptmann Franz Pfeffer von Salomon. The purpose of the NSAK was to mobilize all National Socialist motorists or motor enthusiasts into motoring units whereby the use of their vehicles enabled the SA and other Party formations to be more mobile and to encourage the Party membership to become more motor-minded. Adolf Hühnlein took over the leadership of the NSAK from von Pfeffer when the latter was removed from his post as Oberste Sturmabteilungenführer (OSAF) at the end of 1930. Hühnlein re-organised the NSAK into Motorstandarten, Motorstaffeln and Motorsturme and the membership of the organisation increased correspondingly. The name of the NSAK was officially changed to that of NSKK as from 1 May 1931.

The Motor-SA (MSA) was offically founded on 15 May 1931 but this formation claimed to trace its ancestry back to the small fleet of motor bikes, cars and lorries which the Munich Nazis aquired after 1922 and which, under the leadership of Christian Weber, were used for the purposes of transporting their shock troops and propaganda material. Party members were encouraged to loan to the MSA their own vehicles for varying lengths of time. These were organised into SA and SS Motorsturmen and Motorstaffeln. On 23 August 1934 after the great re-organisation that took place throughout the SA, the Motor-SA was absorbed into the NSKK, losing its separate identity and coming under the leadership of the then NSKK SA-Obergruppenführer Adolf Hünhlein, later to become NSKK-Korpsführer.

With the NSAK becoming the NSKK and the Motor-SA being absorbed into the NSKK three years later, after 30 June 1934 the NSKK was declared a separate branch of the Party, independent of the SA and under the command of the Führer. By this time the membership had grown to 350,000 men and by the end of 1938 it counted some 500,000 members organised within Germany into five Motor Ober-gruppen, Nord, Ost, Süd, West and Mitte. Each of these upper groups contained four to five Motorgruppen, which in turn included five to six Motorstaffeln. These were each in turn sub-divided into six Motorsturme with Truppen and Scharen as sub units. Membership to the NSKK was on a voluntary basis.

The dependence of war and modern industry on mechan-isation and transportation increased the importance of the NSKK. In peace-time the primary function of the NSKK had included the teaching of Nazi ideology, promoting the understanding of the internal combustion engine together with motor mechanics in general and driving instruction all in anticipation of mechanical military campaigns as well as assisting the Police to enforce traffic regulations. During the war the NSKK became a major asset for the Party within Germany and throughout all German-held territories. Its primary war tasks included: the pre-military training of men between the ages of eighteen and forty-five, as well as the Motor-HJ, to ensure the provision of recruits for the motorised and armoured units of the Armed Forces. Train-ing of Army pioneers and assault engineers in the handling of assault boats, a task undertaken by instructors from the Marine-NSKK. Organising NSKK Transport Companies which moved supplies for the Armed Forces and other formations, such as the Organisation Todt (see Fig. 211–213 and 215). These companies provided courier and other road communication services; the training and forming of Trans-port Companies consisting of non-German personnel, in the main of Dutch, Flemings, Walloons and Frenchmen; and finally assisted the Police by forming traffic control and transport control squads. The wartime leader of the NSKK was NSKK-Korpsführer Erwin Kraus.

Once the NSKK had become a separate organisation independent of the SA the rank insignia introduced into the NSKK surprisingly underwent only one change between 1934 and 1945. With only a few exceptions (Figs 31 and 35 being just two) collar patches for the NSKK were black in colour. White metal insignia, including buttons were worn by all ranks including that of NSKK-Korpsführer. Two items of distinctive headdress were used. The black cloth side-cap which after 1936 also displayed the wearer's rank up to and including the rank of NSKK-Haupttruppführer by a system of white metal pips and/or SS pattern silver braiding matching the rank insignia shown on his left hand collar patch (Figs 32 and 35). The second item was the black leather 'Sturzhelm' or crash helmet worn with or without the leather neck flap and displaying the white metal NSKK emblem across the front (Fig. 33 shows the later pattern emblem and Fig. 36 the pre-war early pattern, which, however, continued in use even after the second type had been introduced). Black breeches were a feature of the NSKK uniform and were used even when the earlier Motor-SA existed to distinguish its members from the regular SA personnel. The black and white metal gorget shown in Fig. 35 was known as the 'Verkehrserziehungsdienst Ringkragen' or Traffic Education Service gorget worn by members of the NSKK Traffic Instruction Service when on duty.

37.
II. Marine Brigade Ehrhardt: Non-Commissioned Officer, 1933, Service Dress.

There existed in Germany, in the period immediately following the First World War until mostly absorbed by the SA, a widespread movement of 'illegally' armed bands of men known as 'Freikorps'. Practically all of these bands of nationalist minded volunteers were made up of former front-line soldiers and sailors who had organised themselves at the end of the Great War into armed units to support the Reichswehr in helping to maintain law and order within the Reich and to protect Germany's eastern frontiers against the Poles and the Bolsheviks. One such unit was the extreme right-wing 2nd Marine Brigade Ehrhardt, formed in

Northern Germany and named after its founder and leader Captain Ehrhardt. The Freikorps formations, volunteer detachments, border protection battalions, independent protection battalions, protection regiments and many others to name but a few all existed before the Nazi Party actually amounted to anything. All of them were however to be influenced eventually by the coming of the National Socialists. In many cases the presence of the fast growing Brownshirt battalions proved to be too strong for the smaller Freikorps units and although the purpose for their existence was already on the wane many of them declined rapidly both in numbers and influence with their men going over to Hitler's Movement and joining the SA. Those that were large enough to stay the course and to stand by themselves were eventually to be absorbed by the SA and SS either as individuals or as complete units or they were dissolved altogether by the Nazis once they came to power.

The 2nd Marine Brigade Ehrhardt, in keeping with all other Freikorps and Defence League units, adopted an emblem which was worn as a badge on their uniforms and in many cases was used as a symbol displayed on their unit flags. The Brigade Ehrhardt used for their emblem a Viking raiding ship in full sail set within an oval of twisted rope and bearing the legend 'Ehrhardt'. This grey metal emblem was worn by all ranks of the Brigade on the left upper arm of their tunics (Fig. 37). NCOs were identified by a system of one, two or three silver chevrons worn below the Erhardt Viking ship emblem and Brigade officers were distinguished by wearing one, two, three or four sleeve rings to the cuffs of their tunics. The silver-edged, black cuff-title bearing the double SS silver runes was worn by members of the Brigade Ehrhardt when they were incorporated with the SS. It is a point of interest to note that men from the Brigade Ehrhardt actually formed the very first Adolf Hitler Bodyguard in March 1923. Known as a Stabswache or Headquarters Guard they wore field-grey greatcoats and tunics, black kepis bearing a silver coloured death's head button and black-edged swastika arm bands. This Staff Guard was short lived however and lasted for only two months. It was replaced by a new bodyguard formed by Hitler under the command of Julius Schreck and Joseph Berchtold and was called Stosstrupp Adolf Hitler.

38, 39.
Stahlhelm Veteran Soldiers Organisation: 38) Officer, 1920, Service Dress. 39) Wehrmann and Standard Bearer, 1933, Ceremonial Uniform.

The Stahlhelm or 'Steel Helmet' was a right-wing, nationalist organisation of German ex-servicemen founded by Franz Seldte at Magdeburg on 25 December 1918. Throughout the 1920's and early '30's this formation grew in numbers and units were established in practically every district in Germany. By the time the Nazis came to power the Steel Helmet had developed into the largest of all the ex-servicemen's organisations that existed in Germany. After 30 January 1933 however, the National Socialist German Workers Party was the only political party permitted to exist in Germany and accordingly plans were made to dissolve the Stahlhelm. In March 1933 Franz Seldte became the Reich Labour Minister in the new government and his place as leader of the Stahlhelm was taken by Oberstleutnant Düsterberg, the former acting leader of the organisation. However, it was discovered that Düsterberg's paternal grandfather was a Jew and as Düsterberg was not therefore entitled to call himself an Aryan he was dismissed as Bundesführer of the Stahlhelm. In April of the same year Nazi Party Deputy Leader Hess (Fig. 5) announced that members of the Stahlhelm who wished to join the Nazi Party had first to abandon their Steel Helmet membership. It was also forbidden for a member of the Nazi Party to be a Steel Helmet member. By June 1933 Seldte declared in public that he and his organisation were behind Hitler, that the Kernel Stahlhelm (War Veterans) would remain as before under his leadership but that the 'Scharnhorst Jugend' or young Steel Helmet members over the age of 21 years who had not taken part in the First World War were to be placed under the control of the SA and SS. In July 1933 Hitler issued an order in which he stated that the entire Stahlhelm organisation was placed under the command of the Supreme Leadership of the Sturmabteilung, the SA, and that it would accordingly be reorganised, in other words it ceased to exist as a separate entity. It was formally dissolved in November 1935.

Members of the Stahlhelm wore uniforms of field–grey, based on the field–uniforms as worn during the First World War. They wore a peaked cap with two cockades, leather waist belts and invariably with a leather cross strap. Their emblem was a First World War pattern German steel helmet in profile, hence their name. During the formative period of the organisation their insignia of rank varied from district to district but the most established type was that used on a range of collar patches, shoulder straps not being worn, which continued to be used for a time after the Stahlhelm became the SA first line reserve. These patches displayed a system of small and large oakleaves, thick and thin lace bars and pips which together indicated an ascending system of ranks from Wehrmann (Fig. 39) to Bundesführer. The patches themselves were normally in black with white edging but other colours were used such as pink for motorised units, bright red for leadership assistants, gold–yellow for cavalry troops, dark brown for signals units and cornflower blue for paymaster department. Stahlhelm district badges were worn on the right upper arm of the tunics (Fig. 39 shows the badge for the Greater Berlin Stahlhelm District).

40, 41, 42, 43, 44, 45, 46, 47, 48.
The General-SS: 40) SS-Oberscharführer, SS-Führer-schüle Braunschweig, 1935, Service Dress. 41) Reichs-führer-SS Heinrich Himmler, 1938, Ceremonial Dress. 42) SS-Unterscharführer, 1934, Tradition Uniform. 43) SS-Obersturmführer, 1936, Service Dress. 44) SS-Gruppenführer Reinhard Heydrich, 1938, Greatçoat as Winter Full Dress. 45) SS-Untersturmführer, 1937, Service Dress. 46) SS-Hauptscharführer, 1939, Chancellery Staff Attendants Uniform, 47) SS-Unterscharführer, 1938, Winter Ceremonial Uniform. 48) SS-Obersturmbannführer, 1939, White Summer Full Dress Uniform.

The Allgemeine-SS was often referred to by non-Germans, and still is even today, as Hitler's – or Himmler's – 'Black Shirts'. This is technically incorrect as it was their uniforms that were black and their shirts, by tradition, were brown. The Tradition Uniform (Fig. 42) was the uniform worn at the time when the SS was part of the SA. They differed from the SA in that they wore black kepis with a white metal death's head badge, black ties and black breeches. Their collar insignia was also black. The former SA/SS brown shirt was retained for normal service wear when the SS were uniformed with black tunics and breeches (Fig. 40). Heinrich Himmler was born in Munich on 7 October 1900. He was created Reichsführer-SS in 1929 (Fig. 41), appointed Police President of Bavaria in 1933, Chief of the Reich Political Police in 1935 and Chief of the German Police in 1936. He became Minister of the Interior in 1943, Commander-in-Chief of the Replacement Army in July 1944 and Commander-in-Chief of the Rhine and Vistula Armies in December 1944 until March 1945.

Himmler was dismissed from his position of Reichsführer-SS by Hitler in April 1945 and stripped of his Party membership. In a vain attempt to escape capture and disguised as a German sergeant he was apprehended by the

British on 23 May 1945. He committed suicide later that same day after first revealing his true identity at a British Army Interrogation Centre at Lüneburg.

SS officers from the rank of SS-Sturmführer were appointed as Adjutants by the Reichsführer. Their appointment was indicated by the wearing of an Adjutant's aiguillette, worn across the right chest of the uniform and which, from 1934, was in black and silver. This was later changed to an all silver-aluminium aiguillette. The SS Service Dagger model 1936 with its ornate 'chains' (Fig. 43) was introduced on 25 August 1936 to be worn by commissioned officers and those non-commissioned ranks who were members of the SS before 30 January 1933. It was worn with Service Dress and Undress Uniform. Reinhard Heydrich born in 1904 was head of what developed into the SS Intelligence Service, the Sicherheitsdienst or SD. He was appointed to this job by Himmler in 1931 and he held the appointment until 1934. He was Chief of the Security Police and the SD from 1934 until 1939, Chief of the RSHA (Reichssicherheitshauptamt or Reich Security Main Office) which included the Kripo or Criminal Police and the Gestapo from 1939 until his death in 1942. Heydrich was appointed Reichsprotektor of Bohemia and Moravia in September 1941. On 27 May 1942 two British trained Czech parachutists ambushed Heydrich's car when he was driving through Prague and managed to inflict severe wounds on him which resulted eight days later in his death on 4 June.

The field-grey SS Service Uniform, tunics and greatcoats, identical in cut to the earlier black versions, began to be introduced for use by members of the SD and Security Police during 1938–39 (Fig. 44). In place of the SS swastika arm band the SS version of the National Emblem was worn on the upper left arm and two shoulder cords were worn instead of just one. The basis of the regional organisation of the Allgemeine-SS was the District or Oberabschnitt. These were sub-divided into sub-districts known as Abschnitten. The staffs of these SS-sub-districts wore the number of their

123

sub-district in Roman numerals on their right collar patch and on their cuff-title. Fig. 45 shows an SS–Untersturmführer from the Frankfurt am Oder Abschnitt XII. The use of Army pattern sabres in place of the regulation SS Officers sword (Figs 44 and 48) was not a common practice but it was tolerated during the pre-war period.

SS personnel entrusted with the task of acting as attendants upon Hitler, his guests and members of his immediate staff when the Führer was at the Reich Chancellery in Berlin or at the Berghof at Berchtesgaden wore a short, white 'monkey jacket'. This was always worn with white piped, long black trousers and black leather shoes. Slight variations on the style of jacket shown (Fig. 46) existed and during the war members of Hitler's attending staff wore the SS arm eagle on the left upper arm. SS honour guards wore white leather equipment for ceremonial duties, parades and certain guard duties. Troops of the Leibstandarte Adolf Hitler wore full white leather harness which had 'Y' straps in place of the single cross strap (Fig. 47) when acting as body guard at the Reich Chancellery. The white summer tunic (Fig. 48) was introduced on 27 June 1939 intended to be worn by officers as a Walking-out Uniform when worn with matching regulation white trousers, white buckskin shoes and peaked cap, sometimes with a white top. This white linen tunic was only permitted to be worn during the period from 1 April to 30 September each year. It was known to be worn by the Honour Guard Commander at Berchtesgaden when, in place of the white trousers, he wore black breeches (Fig. 48).

49, 50, 51.
SS–Special Purpose Troops: 49) SS–VT Recruit, 1933, Drill clothing. 50) SS–Obersturmführer, Instructor, 1934, Service Uniform. 51) SS–Untersturmführer, 1934, Service Uniform.

The SS–Verfügungstruppe or SS–Special purpose Troops (SS–VT) was officially brought into existence on 24 September 1934, just three months after armed units of the SS had ruthlessly put down the so-called 'Röhm Plot' (see section on Ernst Röhm, Fig. 17). Full-time Political Readiness Detachments (Politische Bereitschaften) formed for the purpose of police and internal security duties already existed prior to the SS-VT being raised, the most notable detachment of which was the SS-Bodyguard Regiment 'Adolf Hitler' under the command of Joseph 'Sepp' Dietrich. These detachments which were of company strength had in turn been formed from trained units known as 'SS Special Detachments' (SS-Sonderkommandos), later called Kasernierte Hundertschaften (literally 100 men per barracks) and these SS Special Detachments had grown out of the 'Headquarters Guards' (Stabswachen) usually consisting of a hundred armed men that had been raised in certain areas of Germany and in SS Districts (see also Fig. 21). In December 1943 these Political Readiness Detachments were organised into battalions and merged with the 'Leibstandarte Adolf Hitler'. On 16 March 1935 (the date that military conscription was re-introduced in Germany), it was announced publicly that the SS-Verfügungstruppe, the armed body of military trained men, NCOs and Officers, the forerunner of the Armed-SS, yet to be, actually existed.

The light grey drill clothing was produced for wear by NCOs and Men of the SS-VT as a form of protective clothing to be used in place of the black uniform when undergoing military instruction, drill and fatigue duties.

The recruit in Fig. 49 is wearing the first pattern drill clothing worn together with the distinctive field cap. Fig. 50 shows an SS-VT Officer Instructor wearing the drill jacket with black breeches and boots and the officer black peaked cap. The SS-Untersturmführer in Fig. 51 is wearing the earth-grey uniform with the model 1918 black painted steel helmet displaying the first pattern outlined swastika emblem originally worn by all SS-VT units other than the LAH.

125

52.
The Hitler Youth: Reichsjugendführer Artur Axmann, 1942, Full Summer Dress.

Artur Axmann became Reich Youth Leader on 2 August 1940 when he succeeded Baldur von Schirach, the former Reichsjugendführer who was appointed Reichsstatthalter of Vienna. Axmann served for six months with the German Army in Russia between June and December 1941 and it was during this period that he lost his right arm.

During the war and the period preceding the outbreak of war the uniforms of the Hitlerjugend underwent a number of changes. The greatcoat was slightly altered (see Fig. 54) and the uniform peaked cap worn by middle ranking and senior Hitler Youth Leaders was also altered. The former caps (Fig. 54) with cap bands of light brown were replaced by those with a black cap band (Fig. 52); however, both types continued in use for quite some time. The rank insignia in the form of shoulder straps was modified and collar patches were introduced for the rank of Reichsjugendführer. These were of a design identical to those worn by Viktor Lutze as SA Chief-of-Staff (Fig. 23), NSKK-Korpsführer Adolf Hühnlein and by Heinrich Himmler as Reichsführer-SS (Fig. 41). The colours however were different in each case.

53.
The Hitler Youth: Kameradschaftsführer, 1938, Summer Service Dress.

The first attempt to establish a youth section of the National Socialist Movement was started in 1922 with the creation on 13 May of the 'Jugendbund der NSDAP'. As a junior branch of the SA it came under the command of the SA. Members of the youth section wore an almost identical brown uniform to that worn by the SA and this gave rise to certain problems. Many of the older boys of 16 to 18 years of age in the group known as the 'Jungsturm Adolf Hitler' were often involved in street brawls with the political opponents of the Nazis, some even being killed, when they were mistaken for members of the SA. To distinguish the youth section from the adult members of the SA in 1924 the Jungsturm took to wearing a separate uniform with a swastika arm band of a special design (the pattern eventually adopted by the Hitler Youth), different to that of the 'Kampfbinde' worn by the rank and file members of the SA Detachments (Fig. 53). In 1933 the Hitlerjugend was offcially formed as an independent organisation of the NSDAP no longer under the command of the SA. The same year saw the incorporation of all German youth clubs and youth formations into the Hitler Youth with the international Boy Scouts movement being banned in Germany. Baldur von Schirach was appointed Reich Youth Leader. With the passing of the 'Youth Service Law' (Jugenddienstgesetz) on 25 March 1939 service in the Hitler Youth became compulsory for every male and female child in Germany between the ages of ten and eighteen-twenty-one for girls. See sections on the Deutsche Jungvolk (Figs 64–66) and the Bund Deutscher Mädels (Figs 61–63).

For normal summer wear a brown shirt was worn together with a black neckerchief held in place by a brown leather toggle. Black shorts were worn (Lederhosen in Fig. 53) with a leather waist belt and cross strap. Long grey socks and black leather shoes usually completed the outfit. For the purpose of a command structure Germany was divided up into a number of Hitler Youth Districts or HJ-Gebiete. Arm badges in the shape of a triangle were worn on the left upper arm of their shirts or tunics which showed the name of the wearer's HJ District. All Hitler Youth members (males only) were issued with a short-bladed knife, the 'HJ-Fahrtenmesser' or Travelling Knife. This was carried in a metal sheath worn from the waist belt.

54.
The Hitler Youth: Gefolgschaftsführer, 1940, Full Dress Winter Service Uniform.

During the Second World War Hitler Youth Leaders were issued with a mid-brown coloured greatcoat with black lapel facings and dark brown buttons. This differed slightly from the previous pre-war greatcoat which had an all black collar as well as black lapel facings. When worn during the winter months both versions could be used as Undress Winter Uniform by being worn without the waistbelt or with the waistbelt, as shown here in Fig. 54, as Full Dress Winter Service Uniform.

55.
Hitler Youth: Anti-Aircraft Gun Crew Helper, 1944. Special HJ-Flakhelfer Greatcoat.

Flakhelfern were members of the Hitler Youth who volunteered for war work assisting on anti-aircraft gun sites. They served as messengers, signallers, weather observers and ammunition carriers. In some cases they were even employed as gunners, locators and searchlight operators with both anti-aircraft batteries and with gun crews of flak towers.

They wore a special blue-grey uniform consisting of a short battle-dress style blouse and long trousers gathered at the ankles. On this blouse was displayed special insignia together with the familiar HJ arm band. A blue-grey greatcoat and side cap was part of this uniform (Fig. 55).

56.
Hitler Youth: Fire Fighting Hitler Youth Squad Member, 1943, Service Dress.

Special fire fighting squads were organised in those German towns and cities that had large numbers of industrial concerns and which were being increasingly bombed by the Allies as the war progressed. These squads which supplemented the regular fire police brigades were made up of volunteers from the Hitler Youth who were aged fifteen years and over. They were distinguished by a special diamond shaped badge worn on the lower left cuff of their tunic which incorporated the Hitler Youth emblem set against a background of carmine red flames. They wore khaki brown uniforms with a black side cap on which was displayed a police-eagle cap emblem.

57.
Hitler Youth: Special Patrol Service Youth Member, 1943, Winter Service Uniform.

The Hitlerjugend Streifendienst was a special patrol service consisting of older members of the Hitler Youth. It was set up for the purpose of policing the Hitler Youth but during the later stages of the war years it became an armed body of fanatical youth members who assisted the Police and the SS in hunting down escaped prisoners of war, allied aircrews who had baled out of their aircraft and anyone else that was suspected of evading the authorities or were considered as enemy agents working against the Nazi regime.

They wore the standard pattern HJ uniforms and were distinguished by the use of a special cuff-title bearing the words 'HJ Streifendienst' together with white piping to their shoulder straps. When on patrol service they wore a special Streifendienst gorget.

They were trained to use small arms and rifles and carried rifles when on duty.

58, 59, 60.
The Hitler Youth, Naval Branch: 58) Marine-Hitlerjugend 1939, Marine-HJ Winter Service Dress. 59) Marine-HJ Bannführer 1942, Summer Full Dress Uniform. 60) Marine-Hitlerjugend 1936, White Working Rig.

The naval branch of the Hitler Youth movement was created to foster and promote an interest in ships and sailing. Boys from coastal areas around Germany and those parts of Germany near large expanses of inland water and waterways were encouraged to join these Marine-HJ units. When membership of the HJ became compulsory in 1939 these naval units became a valuable means of teaching these youngsters the art of seamanship in preparation for their possible or eventual entry into the regular war-time Kriegsmarine.

Many aspects of the uniforms worn by members of the Marine-HJ were based on those uniforms to be found in the German Navy. However, the most notable difference was the use of white metal insignia and fittings in place of the gilt coloured items used by the Kriegsmarine, and for that matter the Marine-SA. The leadership of the Marine-HJ was furnished by qualified older youths or adults, normally acting as instructors (Fig. 59). Their uniform was very similar to that worn by members of the Marine-SA (see Fig. 30). Shoulder straps worn by members of the Marine-HJ which were the only systematic visual method employed to indicate rank differed from the final pattern shoulder straps used by the rest of the Hitler Youth and introduced during 1938. The Marine-HJ shoulder straps were of dark navy-blue piped yellow whereas the rest of the HJ were in black and piped in various colours according to their branch of HJ service, as follows:

Allgemeine-HJ (General HJ) in bright red, Motor-HJ (Motorised HJ) in pink, Flieger-HJ (Aviation HJ) in light blue, Nachrichten-HJ (Signals HJ) in lemon yellow, HJ-

Streifendienst (Special Patrol Service HJ) white (see Fig.57), also NPEA (National Political Education Institutes) in white (see Fig. 85), Landjahr-HJ (One Year Land Service HJ) in green and finally Gebietsstäbe/RJF (District Staff and Reichs Youth Leader Staff HQ's) in crimson.

61, 62, 63.
The Hitler Youth – League of German Girls: 61) BDM-Mädelringführerin, 1940, Work Clothing. 62) BDM-Reichsreferentin Dr Jutta Rüdiger, 1939, Service Uniform for Summer Wear. 63) BDM-Mädelgruppenführerin, 1943, Summer Dress.

The Bund Deutsche Mädels – BDM – was part of the Hitler Youth. It was organised into three sub-divisions. The BDM proper for girls and young women from the age of 14 years up to 21, the Jungmädels (JM) for girls from 10 years to 14 years and the BDM Glaube und Schönheit (Faith and Beauty) for young women from 17 to 21 years of age.

The first two categories of girls were uniformed and wore regulation issue clothing. The organisation of the BDM was divided up into units varying in size and covering the whole Reich including the annexed and occupied territories. Ranks were used and these depended on a girl's age and her accepted responsibility. In 1939 service in the Hitler Youth, which included the BDM became compulsory. In the decree published on 25 March 1939 it was stated that all sixteen to eighteen year old Hitlerjugend were to perform annual public service; boys were encouraged to work on the land at harvest time and girls to help families with large numbers of children. The 'Landdienst' or Land Service first instituted in 1934 grew in size each year. Both boys and especially girls were encouraged and expected to volunteer for service on farms for a one year period. During the war both the annual harvest help and the one year Land Service became an important contribution to the German war effort. The one year Land Service was marked by the wearing on the BDM (and Hitler Youth) uniform of a black cuff-title with the white lettering 'Landdienst der HJ (Fig. 61 and Fig. 53). Rank in the BDM was indicated on the dark blue uniform and the white summer blouse by a series of graduated cloth badges, the most senior of which is shown in Fig. 62. Multi-coloured lanyards were also worn and these too showed the wearer's BDM or JM rank (Fig. 63). One of the most commonly worn items of uniform was the BDM Kletterjacke or BDM climbing jacket. Made from light brown coloured suedette material with leather or brown plastic 'football patterned' buttons (Fig. 236).

64, 65, 66.
The Hitler Youth – Junior Section (Boys): 64) DJ 'Pimpf', 1942, Winter Service Uniform. 65) DJ-Oberjungzugführer, 1943, Winter Service Uniform. 66) DJ-Jungzugführer, 1934, Summer Uniform.

The male side of the Hitler Youth was divided into two sections, the Hitler Youth proper made up of boys from 14 years to youths of 18 years and the Deutsche Jungvolk or DJ consisting of boys from the age of 10 to 14 (see also section on BDM, Figs 61, 62, 63).

Winter Uniform for the DJ, depending on the boys age, consisted of black shorts or long dark blue trousers worn with either the dark blue tunic or the dark blue blouse with large collar. Under this was worn a light brown shirt and black neckerchief held in place by a brown leather toggle. For summer wear the tunic was left off and shorts were worn. Members of the DJ wore only a single shoulder strap on the right shoulder of their tunics and blouse. It was black with a black edging and showed the number of the DJ unit in white cotton.

67, 68, 69, 70, 71, 72, 73, 74, 75.
National Socialist Volunteer Labour Service and National Labour Service: 67) Musician Freiwillige Arbeiter, 1931, Service Dress. 68) Feldmeister, 1932, Service Uniform. 69) Arbeiter, 1932, Winter Work Uniform. 70) Truppführer, Musician, 1937, Service Dress. 71) Unterfeldmeister 1936, Service Dress. 72) Arbeitsführer, 1937, Formal Dress. 73) Obervormann, 1943, Field Service Uniform. 74) Reichsarbeitsführer Konstantin Hierl, 1940, Parade Uniform. 75) Arbeitsarzt, 1944, Greatcoat.

The Reichsarbeitsdienst, the National Labour Service (RAD) had developed from an earlier Nazi Party organisation first set up in 1931 and known as the NS-Freiwillige Arbeitsdienst or National Socialist Volunteer Labour Service (Figs 67, 68 & 69). This early Nazi formation was just one of many organisations created at that time to try and ease the unemployment amongst Germany's youth. In July 1931, in an effort to alleviate the problem of widespread unemployment, the Brüning Government passed a law which allowed the setting up of work camps to house volunteers who undertook to perform volunteer labour service.

In an effort to counter their political rivals the Nazis proceeded to organise their own camps. The first Volunteer Labour Service camp was mustered at Hammerstein in the Grenzmark District. A few months later the Free State of Anhalt made such labour service State-wide. In 1929 Konstantin Hierl had been appointed by Hitler charged with the responsibility of creating a nation-wide labour service organised along military lines. Hierl had been a professional soldier with over thirty years military service. He had served as Director of the War Academy in Munich and later at the War Ministry in Berlin. During the Spartacist troubles he had raised the 'Hierl Detachment' and driven the Socialists out of Augsburg. His Nationalist sympathies were beyond doubt and he was considered an ideal choice for this task. Hierl's

133

conception of German Labour Service however went far beyond the need to counter unemployment. His Labour Service was to be a cardinal feature in the building of the New Germany. The idea behind it all was that manual labour provided the means of breaking down social and class barriers, moulding the character of the young and reviving interest in the dignity of manual labour. 'Labour service' Hierl claimed 'shall be the proud privilege of German Youth and shall be service to the whole Volk.'

In 1933 Konstantin Hierl was appointed by Hitler as Secretary of State for Labour Service. After much experimentation and delays, caused in part by foreign protests against what was regarded as thinly veiled military conscription, steps were taken in the summer of 1934 to introduce universal and obligatory labour service. On 26 June 1935 the Reich Labour Service Law was passed making service in the RAD both nation-wide and compulsory. The RAD ceased to be a Party organisation and instead was created a Supreme Reich Authority, a state organisation on a par with the other Reich ministeries. Hierl, as Reichsarbeitsführer (Fig. 74) became a member of the Party's Reichsleitung as a Secretary of State. From this date, 26 June 1935, all male Aryan Germans between the ages of 17 and 25 years had to serve in the RAD for six months, which once the machinery got under way became six months labour service prior to induction into the Armed Forces. In peace-time the RAD was instrumental in the construction of the Autobahn system as well as other roads. They undertook land reclamation, drainage projects and soil conservation work. Much of their work was however of a military nature.

At the outbreak of war the RAD became an important auxiliary of the German Armed Forces. It formed the nucleus of the construction battalions of the Army and Air Force. To begin with such battalions were formed by the outright conversion of the RAD units into pioneer groups with an average strength of 2,000 men and consisting of four construction companies and three construction columns.

They served in the Polish Campaign of 1939 during which they helped construct fortifications, roads and airfields, carried out repairs to railways, brought up supplies, collected and sorted captured equipment, guarded prisoners and helped with the Polish harvest. In December 1939 the RAD reverted to its original rôle and from then on for the rest of the war continued to carry out its war-time duties under its own commanders and under RAD rules and administration. By 1943 the men of the RAD were fully armed and had become completely militarised (Fig. 73). They now performed, in addition to their construction work and labouring, the task of laying minefields and manning fortifications. They were taught anti-tank and anti-aircraft defence duties. By 1944 conditions within Germany had worsened to such an extent that it made it necessary for the RAD to be employed in operating anti-aircraft batteries. One of their primary functions during this period was to help in fire-fighting, the construction of air raid shelters and temporary accommodation for the bombed-out and the clearing of bomb damage.

The RAD was active in all German-held territory and in many instances individual RAD units remaining in the field or finding themselves in German areas which became parts of the combat zone were often absorbed into the Wehrmacht usually to fight as infantry. In 1939 it was estimated that the membership of the RAD stood at 360,000 men. This number decreased rapidly and was considerably less at the end of the war.

The early FAD uniforms were in many ways similar to the uniforms of the RAD. The basic uniform colour of earth brown was used by both organisations as was the facing and piping colour of dark, or chocolate brown, both colours having an obvious association with earth and soil. The system of rank insignia developed from the Volunteer Labour Service's use of simple silver on black collar patches and shoulder straps (Fig. 68), through the introduction in 1936 of the red and white design on black collar patches to the

135

use in 1940 of new insignia; the shoulder straps remaining the same (Figs 70, 71, 72). By 1940 and again in 1943 this rank insignia had undergone another change. The appearance of the shoulder straps was more military, the collar patches were modified (Figs 73, 74) and new branch colours were made use of, notably dark bottle green for RAD Administration personnel and Cornflower blue for Medical troops (Fig. 75). Musicians in the RAD wore 'Swallows nests' the design on the braiding of which was unique to them. The universal use of the 'spade' arm badge, first introduced when the RAD was founded, continued in use right up to the end. (Figs 71, 72, 73, 74, 75). A limited number of cuff-titles were worn in the RAD (Figs 71, 72), the most colourful being the 'Anhalt' cuff-title. This title combined the state colours of Anhalt of red and green and which, worn by selected units, commemorated the fact that Free State Anhalt, very much in sympathy with the Nazi cause, had been the first German state to introduce labour service on a state-wide basis (Fig. 71).

76, 77, 78.
National Labour Service – Women's Section: 76) Arbeitsmaid, 1942, Work Clothing. 77) RADwJ Jungführerin, 1939, Service Uniform. 78) RADwJ Maidenführerin, 1941, Service Uniform.

The Reichsarbeitsdienst der weiblichen Jugend – RADwJ – was the Women's (Female Youth) section of the RAD. Girls entered the RADwJ from the BDM and after completing a six month period of service were normally released. However, under the war-time emergency conditions they were obliged to remain in the RADwJ for the duration. In the main their tasks included: work in factories and munitions plants; workers as auxiliary agricultural labour force (Fig. 76); to assist in various National Socialist war relief agencies; service in hospitals and schools and to help maintain the public utilities and transportation systems (see Fig. 235).

The Service uniforms as worn by the members of the RADwJ were in the same earth brown colour with the same chocolate brown collar as were used by the RAD.

79, 80, 81.
German Labour Front: 79) DAF-Gauwerksscharführer, 1938, Service Dress. 80) Werksscharführer als politische Leiter, 1943, Service Dress. 81) DAF-Spielmann, 1940, Service Dress.

Under the leadership of Reichsleiter Dr Robert Ley (see Fig. 10) the German Labour Front or Deutsche Arbeitsfront – DAF – was set up immediately after the Nazi Party had declared illegal and abolished all Trade Unions throughout Germany. Membership of these outlawed trade unions was forbidden, their property and funds were seized and those workers considered acceptable were compelled to become part of the new State Labour organisation. Membership of the DAF was open to corporate entities as well as individual Aryan workers who had to pay about one and a half per cent of their monthly wages as dues. The Labour Front was so devised as to parallel the structure of the NSDAP itself. It consisted of the NSBO (the Nationalsozialistische Betriebs-organisation) responsible for the political work and guidance of the DAF, the NSHAGO (NS-Handels und Gewerbe-organisation) representing salaried employees, the Reichs-nährstand or Food Estate representing agriculture, the Reich Culture Chamber, the Association of NS German Jurists, the thirteen Trustees of Labour (Treuhänder der Arbeit), the leaders of the twelve groups of the Reichsstand der Industrie, the Organisation of German Industrialists and the Gauleiters of the Party. Its organisation reached from the Zentralbüro controlled by the Leiter der Deutschen Arbeits-front Dr Ley down through Gau, Kreis and Ortsgruppen levels to the smallest factory trade cell (Betriebszellen) led by a Betriebsführer or Trade Unit Leader.

The purpose of the DAF was to ensure the political

stability and trouble-free running of German industry and commerce. The Werksscharen were intended to act as a form of shop steward but as they were required to be ardent National Socialists in reality they proved to be the watchdogs of the Party in checking any disharmony or discontent amongst the workforce at source.

In November 1933 dark blue uniforms together with emblems were provided for all members of the Arbeitsfront which had to be obtained at the expense of the members. Rank was indicated by a series of arm chevrons. Silver for lower ranks and gold for the more senior positions. Four colours were adopted to indicate various State levels for the DAF Werksscharführer; yellow for DAF Oberst-Werksscharführer; red for DAF Gau-Werksscharführer (Fig. 79); black for DAF Kreis-Werksscharführer and light blue for DAF Haupt-Werksscharführer and DAF Werksscharführer. These four colours were used as piping to the shoulder straps and for the coloured lanyards worn on the uniform (Fig. 79).

82, 83, 84.
National Socialist Flying Corps: 82) NSFK-Sturmmann, 1935, Service Dress. 83) NSFK-Standartenführer, 1942. 84) NSFK-Truppführer as Standard Bearer, 1940, Tradition Uniform.

The Nationalsozialistisches Fliegerkorps (NSFK) was a para-military organisation that took the place of the Deutsche Luftsportverband (see Figs 124, 126) when the latter was dissolved in 1935. The NSFK was a State-registered corporation subordinate to the Reich Minister for Air and Commander-in-Chief German Air Force; its Korpsführer Generaloberst Alfred Keller was an active Luftwaffe General directly responsible to Göring. The NSFK was not a Party formation as such but its members enjoyed the same privileges as those of the other para-military organisations, although its members were not permitted to have any other

Party affiliations. The NSFK was partly financed by voluntary contributions from private individuals. Its principal task was to make all Germans air-minded and to stress the rôle of air power in modern warfare. Its war-time functions were mainly as follows:

1) Maintaining schools to train pilots, wireless operators, glider troops and parachutists, as well as other specialised personnel.

2) Giving instruction to the Flieger-HJ.

3) Producing a constant flow of skilled personnel for the Luftwaffe thereby functioning as a reserve pool for them.

Not unexpectedly and no doubt due to its close association with the German Air Force, the NSFK wore uniforms produced in one of the 'protected uniform colours', namely Air Force blue-grey. However, it was very unlikely that members of the NSFK were ever mistaken, at least by Germans, for members of the Luftwaffe. Their badges of rank, shoulder straps and collar patches, were those patterned on the political fashion. They wore blue-grey kepis (Figs 82, 83) and a yellow or silver piped blue-grey beret or 'Dienstmütze' (Fig. 84). The facing colour used only as piping and underlay was bright yellow. The NSFK emblem consisting of Icarus the bird-man of Greek legend with outstretched arms holding wings and overlaid with a black swastika appeared on their uniforms, flags, standards and certain items of regalia. This emblem in cloth form was originally worn for a short time on the right upper arm of the NSFK Service Tunic (Fig. 82) but was later moved so as to be worn above the right breast pocket of the tunic and on the traditional brown shirt (Figs 83, 84).

85, 86, 87.
National Socialist Leadership Schools: 85) NPEA Jungmann, 1943, Walking-Out Uniform. 86) NPEA Instructor, 1935, Service Dress. 87) NPEA Honour Guard, 1940, Guard Uniform.

German children, regardless of class, social origin or family background, other than those who were Jews or of Jewish origin, and who showed at an early age what the Nazis considered to be 'promising material' were selected to be trained in special schools as the future generation of German leaders. This training of the new elite was carried out on a three-tier system. First the 'Nationalpolitische Erziehungs- sanstalten' or NPEA, more commonly referred to as the NAPOLAS (which is the subject dealt with here) with entry at the age of ten, together with the 'Adolf Hitler Schulen' or AHS, entrance age twelve. Secondly the 'Ordensburgen' or Castles Order of (see Fig. 13) entrance age of 24 to 27 and lastly the 'Hohe Schule' of the NSDAP, enrolment of students in their late 20's early 30's onwards.

The NAPOLAS was designed to produce an elite of 'Political Soldiers' capable of filling any post within all spheres of German life. The functioning of the NAPOLAS was based on the methods of the former Imperial German Army Officer Cadet training institutes. The emphasis at these Kadettenanstalten was on soldierly behaviour and military tradition and so it was with the NAPOLAS. The first three NPEAs were founded on 20 April 1933 on Hitler's forty-fourth birthday and by 1944 there was a total of forty-two in Greater Germany with two Reichsschulen the name given to the foreign NPEAs in Holland and one in Belgium.

From 1936 on NPEA pupils had to be members of the HJ or DJ. The organisational structure of these schools was modelled on that of the Army. School forms were known as 'platoons', the pupils were called 'Jungmänner'. Schools carried out military style drills (Fig. 87) and field exercises. Emphasis was placed on educational and scientific training, on character moulding and especially on physical education. From 1940 the NPEAs were becoming heavily influenced by the SS and by late in the war some of the schools were kitted out with Waffen-SS style uniforms (Fig. 85) bearing the SS sleeve eagle.

88.
German Army: Generalfeldmarschall Gerd von Rundstedt, 1945.

Commander-in-Chief of the German Forces in the West and 'Chief' of Infantry Regiment 18, von Rundstedt is shown here wearing a slightly modified version of the Officers Piped Field Service Tunic. In place of the collar patches that were normally worn by an Army Field Marshal (see Fig. 91) von Rundstedt favoured wearing Parade Uniform style collar patches that were normally worn by Infantry officers below the rank of General. This practice, together with the use of shoulder strap numerals 18, emphasised his honorary appointment as a 'Regimental Chief'. He carries his Field-Marshals 'interim-stab', the everyday version of his Field Marshals batton.

89.
German Army: Generalleutnant Seifert, 1939.

First brought into use on 29 June 1935, the Uniform Tunic or Waffenrock, together with trousers or breeches of a special shade of grey were worn by all Army personnel with only rank insignia and colour of buttons to distinguish between Men and Officers. As its name indicates this was the parade style uniform and up to the outbreak of war it was worn as a matter of course on all ceremonial occasions, on important military parades and as a Walking-out Uniform. After September 1939 its use was curtailed and no new issues were made to Men and NCOs. The colour of the Generals cap insignia was changed from silver (Fig. 89) to gold (Fig. 88) on 1 January 1943.

90.
German Army Hauptmann, Infantry Regiment 'Grossdeutschland', 1939.

A specially designed uniform jacket was proposed for use by

141

Soldiers, NCOs and Officers of the German Army's elite Infantry Regiment 'Grossdeutschland'. Introduced in March 1939 it was intended to be worn throughout the Regiment from 15 September 1939. The tunic had two notable features that were unique in German military sartorial art of this period. The cuffs displayed 'French Cuffs', a feature of the uniforms of the former Imperial Garde Schützen Bataillon and the 2.Garde-Maschinengewehr-Abteilung. The collar insignia were of a special elongated design similar to the 'doppellitzen' worn by the elite regiments of the old Imperial German States. Worked in flat aluminium wire with dark green silk for troops and in embroidered aluminium wire for officers these collar 'Litzen' were sewn on to, or worked directly into, the dark blue-green of the collar without the usual underlay of Waffenfarbe cloth.

Due to the outbreak of war the universal issue of these jackets to members of the Regiment was suspended for the duration and only those items that had been manufactured and issued before September 1939 were actually brought into use.

91.
German Army: Generalfeldmarschall Wilhelm Keitel, 1942.

The greatcoat was a garment worn throughout the German Army by all ranks from Private up to and including Field Marshal. Its basic colouring, design and cut were the same for all ranks with only slight variations appearing in those garments worn by Officers and Generals who normally purchased their own, individually tailored, greatcoats usually made from fine quality materials. The greatcoat was correctly worn buttoned at the neck but exceptions were permitted, notably those persons who had received the Knight's Cross or who were officers of the rank of General or above and Administration Officials of a corresponding status. In the case of the Knight's Cross holder the collar of

142

his greatcoat was worn open at the neck to display its neck decoration and for Generals and Field Marshals (Fig. 91), Administrative Officials and Army Clergy the lapels were turned back to reveal their red, dark green or violet facings respectively.

92.
German Army: Generalstab Major, 1940.

The Army officers 'New Style Summer Jacket' shown here was first introduced by an order dated 9 July 1937 and was intended to replace the earlier 'Old Style Reichsheer' white tunic. Both models however continued to be worn for a number of years after this date. The new jacket, worn without white trousers – these did not exist – was prescribed for wear, weather permitting, from 1 April to 30 September each year and could be worn on the following occasions:
1) as a Walking-out Uniform;
2) as an ordinary Dress Uniform when worn in the officers mess or officers club, or for social family gatherings or garden parties;
3) at gymnastic, running and sports meetings within Germany and abroad, both for participating in the events and as a spectator.
Rank was only indicated on these jackets by the use of detachable shoulder straps. Collar patches were not used. The detachable buttons and the pin-on national emblem were in silver-white metal for officers and gilt metal for Generals and above including Administrative Officials of a similar status. The buttons, breast emblem and straps were removable to allow for washing the jacket.

93.
German Army: Tank Crew Member, Gefreiter, 1940.

A specially designed uniform was introduced into the German Army to be worn by all those personnel serving in armoured fighting vehicles. It was unique in that nothing quite like it had been used before. It was intended as both a Dress Uniform (Fig. 93) and for field service use as a Service Uniform. It was well suited for use within the confined space of an armoured vehicle. Being made of strong black material it tended not to show grease and oil stains; a common occurrence with crews of armoured vehicles. The jacket was short which gave ease of movement and was double breasted which afforded extra protection to the wearer when on the move during cold weather. It had no cuffs, no external buttons and the shoulder straps were usually stitched flat on to the shoulders of the jacket. This all meant that it was less likely to get caught up on any projections within the vehicle. Initially a black, cloth beret which covered a lightweight crash helmet was issued to these Panzer troops to be worn with this uniform but this was soon withdrawn in favour of a black side cap. Armoured personnel wore the standard pattern field-grey steel helmet.

94.
German Army: Oberintendanturrat, 1938, Full Dress Uniform.

The German Army Full Dress Uniform, the 'Grosser Gesellschaftanszug', consisted of the uniform tunic worn without the officers silver and green brocade parade belt (see Figs 89 & 90) but with officers silver parade aiguillettes, long piped trousers, black half shoes, gloves, uniform peaked cap, medals or ribbons, decorations and dagger. The Oberintendanturrat or Commissariat Lieutenant-Colonel illustrated here wears gold coloured 'Kurbelstickerei' embroidered on to the dark green of his collar patches and cuff-facing patches and which are piped bright red as his second or 'Neben-waffenfarbe'.

95.
German Army: Feldbischof, 1937, Frock Coat.

The frock coat was an item of dress peculiar to the German Army Clergy. Chaplains (Heerespfarrer), Senior Chaplains (Heeresoberpfarrer) and Field Bishops (Feldbischöfe) were all permitted to wear this over garment as an alternative to their violet lapelled greatcoat and the Army officers cloak. The Army clergy were unique in that they wore no shoulder straps on any of their military dress and on the frock coat collar patches were also not worn. It was only by the use of gold coloured buttons, cap cords, cap piping and the national emblem in gold was it possible to distinguish Field Bishops from Chaplains and Senior Chaplains. They wore white metal buttons and silver aluminium cap cords and national emblem.

96.
German Army: Hauptwachtmeister – 13. Kavallerie-Regiment, 1939, Walking-out Uniform.

The walking-out uniform worn by non-commissioned officers and men of the German Army consisted of the Service Tunic worn with long trousers, black half shoes, peaked cap and with or without waist belt. Medals or ribbon bars and decorations together with marksmanship lanyards were worn as was a side arm, either a bayonet and scabbard for men and NCOs or a sabre for Cavalry NCOs. The plain grey coloured trousers were a feature of German Army uniform dress that was abolished at the beginning of the war and thereafter only trousers or breeches of a field-grey colouring that matched the wearer's tunic were worn. The small white metal skull and cross bones badge worn on the front of the cap between the national emblem and the oakleaf wreath was known as a 'Tradition Badge'. Three types of tradition badges existed in the German Army of this period, all of a differing design. All were worn on the peaked cap in this manner as well as other forms of soft headdress by members of certain selected Army units that were considered to be the inheritors of historical military traditions of former Army regiments.

97, 99.
German Army: 97) Obergefreiter, 1943 Model Service Dress, 1943. 99) Kraftfahrer, M44 Uniform, 1944.

By the year 1943 conditions had become so difficult within Germany that economies were being made in every direction where it was felt that both materials and labour could be conserved. One aspect of this conservation drive was the production first of the Model 1943 Service Tunic and then the Model 1944 Uniform.

The M43 tunic did away with the familiar blue-green collar as well as the backing cloth used for both the national emblem and the shoulder straps. The patch pockets were usually without pleats and the pocket flaps were cut straight (Fig. 97).

On 25 September 1944 the Model 1944 or M44 uniform was introduced (Fig. 99). This was a complete departure in style from anything that the Army had produced up to this time. The blouse to the uniform was in appearance some-what similar to the battle dress blouse worn by the British Army. The most obvious feature of this new style of blouse was the absence of a jacket 'skirt'. This had been done away with and in its place was a waist band 12 cm. deep. Without the normal skirt to the jacket the external pockets on the M44 blouse were reduced to just two. Both these were without pleats and had straight cut pocket flaps. An economy style national emblem was manufactured for use with this blouse. Triangular in shape it required less time to sew to the blouse than did the former emblem. The whole uniform was manufactured in low quality slate-grey cloth, yet another departure from the traditional field-grey of the Army uniforms. The Trousers worn with the M44 Blouse were introduced during 1943 and were worn with both the M43 tunic and M44 blouse. They too were an economy measure. They had a belted waist band at the back, which did away with the need for braces (suspenders). The legs of the trousers were tapered so as to fit into gaiters or tops of ankle boots. Gaiters made from canvas and reinforced with leather were copied directly from the gaiters worn by the British forces. Their introduction helped to conserve the dwindling stock of leather used in the manufacture of footwear. Marching boots (Fig. 97) were phased out and new recruits were issued with or unserviceable boots were replaced by leather ankle boots worn with gaiters or puttees (Figs 98 & 99).

98.
German Army: Grenadier, 1944. Combat clothing and equipment.

The appearance of the average German infantryman during the last two years of the war compared to what he looked like in 1939 had greatly changed. Although the basic weaponry had changed little with only a number of new introductions in the field of small arms taking place and the equipment he wore being much the same as that that had been in use five years previously, it was more the manner in which it was worn and the soldier's general bearing that marked him as a battle-hardened veteran.

Helmet netting was used to break up the hard outline of the steel helmet and at the same time afford a means of camouflaging the soldier's head and shoulders. This idea was copied from the Allies, to supplement the German Army's own steel helmet cloth covers.

A suit of lightweight combat clothing consisting of a four pocket jacket and plain, standard pattern trousers manufactured in a reed-green 'herringbone' pattern drill proved a popular form of issue clothing for those troops fighting during the summer months in temperate climate zones. Both items were worn separately just as often as a complete outfit. Illustrated here (Fig. 98) the soldier wears reed-green trousers combined with the standard pattern field-grey tunic.

100.
German Army: Feldgendarmerie Soldat, 1941.

Tropical clothing was worn not only by troops of the Afrikakorps but also by German forces in southern Russia, Italy, Sicily, Greece and those Mediterranean and hot climate countries occupied by the Axis and where German troops were garrisoned. In the main the lightweight clothing was manufactured from tan coloured material but constant washing, the effects of sun and desert air tended to bleach this colour out to a nondescript shade of off white.

The Field Police soldier shown here on foot patrol (Fig. 100) is wearing the Tropical Sun Helmet, an item of military headdress that was short lived and was replaced by the tropical version of the Replacement Field Cap. Around his neck and the neck of the NCO in Figure 102 is hung the 'Feldgendarmerie' (Military Field Police) duty gorget.

101.
German Army: Hauptwachtmeister Self-Propelled Artillery Unit, 1944.

With the advent of self-propelled artillery it was found necessary to introduce yet another new uniform. When designing the uniform for crews of tank destroyers and self-propelled assault guns serving in Panzer and Panzer-grenadier divisions with their need for close observation work both inside and away from their armoured vehicles, it was decided to use the same style and practical cut of the special black Panzer Uniform (Fig. 93) but to produce this new version in field-grey material to give better camouflage qualities.

102.
German Army: Feldgendarmerie Feldwebel, 1942.

The use of the motorcycle in the German Armed Forces was widespread. Army reconnaissance units as well as individual dispatch riders used motorcycles, either single machines or with side-car combinations, but without the protection of leg guards or windshield riding a machine in wet, cold or muddy conditions was an uncomfortable business. The rubberised, waterproof motorcycle coat was specifically designed for use by motorcyclists to afford them some protection against the elements although drivers of other vehicles and especially those without the protection of an enclosed cab, made use of it. The sergeant-major shown on traffic control duty is wearing the special cold weather felt overboots.

103.
German Army: Grenadier (Sniper), 1943, Reversible Winter Uniform.

When the Germans invaded Russia in 1941 it was during the height of the summer months. By October when the first snows of the winter began to fall the Germans were far from having obtained their expected victory over the Soviet Forces, and they were still outside the gates of Moscow when winter set in in earnest. Temperatures, helped by driving winds, plummeted down to 30, 35 even 40 degrees below freezing. Without adequate cold weather clothing the troops suffered enormous numbers of casualties from frost bite and gangrene. The wounded more often than not died of shock from the cold. Men quite literally froze to death where they stood or lay.

Great effort was made throughout Germany during this first Russian winter to try and obtain warm clothing for the troops. Dr Goebbels launched a drive to encourage the German people to hand into collection points any item of clothing, silk, woollen, and especially fur, that could be used by the troops at the front in an effort to protect them from the cold.

By the time the second winter of 1942–43 came around the German Army was better prepared. The reversible winter uniform had been devised, manufactured in time and distributed to the troops. It proved to be a very practical garment consisting of a padded jacket with hood, padded overtrousers and mittens. It kept the soldier warm, it allowed him to spend longer periods out in the open away from the warmth and protection of his bunker or billet and above all it was camouflaged, white for use in snow on one side and multicoloured in greens and browns on the reverse side. (Fig. 103).

104.
German Army: Infantry Feldwebel, 1945, Field Service Uniform.

As the war progressed and the fighting – at first on one, then two and finally on three fronts became more widespread and bitter more and more troops performed increasingly greater numbers of heroic or daring acts of military courage or grim determination. This was reflected in turn by new awards being created and existing awards being upgraded, both in an effort to acknowledge these acts of heroism or service. One such award was the special badge for the single-handed destruction of a tank. Each award in the silver grade represented one enemy tank destroyed single-handedly by the recipient without the aid of an anti-tank weapon. The Feldwebel in Fig. 104 is wearing three such awards, one above the other, positioned on his right upper arm. He also wears the Iron Cross 2nd Class ribbon and the Russian Front ribbon in his tunic button hole, the Iron Cross 1st Class and War Merit Cross in silver with swords 1st Class both pinned to his breast pocket.

105.
German Army: Major, German Mountain Troops, 1940, Field Service Uniform.

German Army Gebirgstruppen or Mountain Troops wore certain items of military dress, in addition to regulation issue items, that were peculiar to them: the Gerbirgsmütze or Mountain Cap with its short cloth peak, windproof anoraks, and various types of trousers especially adapted for use with mountaineering and climbing boots. They were further distinguished by wearing a white metal badge in the form of the Edelweiss flower on the left side of their Gerbirgsmütze, a similar emblem worn on the front of their Uniform Peaked Cap set between the national emblem and the oakleaf wreath, and a cloth Edelweiss arm badge worn on the right upper sleeve of the Field Tunic, Uniform Tunic and Greatcoat.

106, 107, 108.
German Army Female Auxiliaries: 106) Führerin, 1940, Working Dress, summer wear. 107) Oberstabsfüherin, 1941, Walking-out Uniform. 108) Vorhelferin, 1943, Office Dress Overalls.

The 'Nachrichtenhelferinnen des Heeres' was a signals service of the German Army specifically formed for work within Army establishments. It employed women volunteers trained in wireless, telegraph communications work and able to operate telephone switchboards. These women wore regulation issue uniforms consisting of grey uniform jackets and skirts – generally for outdoors use and white blouses and grey overalls for office work, hence their nick-name of 'grey mice'. They were issued with a regulation black leather handbag, but no raincoat. Only the regulation black leather shoes were permitted to be worn when in uniform and no gloves other than black or grey. Only grey stockings (Figs 107 & 108) or white socks (Fig.

151

106) were allowed depending on the uniform being worn. There was a hierarchy of ranks from the lowest non-commissioned rank of Vorhelferin (Fig. 108) up to the most senior commissioned rank of Oberstabsführerin (Fig. 107). Their facing colour used as piping and trimming was yellow. The 'Blitz' emblem was carried on their left upper arm and on the left side of their grey side-caps. A black and silver enamelled 'Blitz' brooch was worn at the throat to indicate a qualified signals operator.

109.
German Navy: Grossadmiral Karl Dönitz, 1944, Grand Admiral's Greatcoat.

All ranks of the German Navy from Warrant Officers up, including junior Midshipmen, wore the naval greatcoat. Like the German Army, the naval greatcoat was worn correctly when it was buttoned up to the neck. However, those naval personnel who were the recipients of neck orders and in the case of Admirals, General Admirals and Grand Admirals, who displayed cornflower blue facings to their greatcoat lapels, they were permitted to wear the collar of the coat open and their lapels turned back.

Kapitän zur See, Karl Dönitz, had taken over the command of the German submarine arm on 1 October 1935. On 1 October he rose to the rank of Admiral and on 30 January 1943 Hitler promoted him to Grossadmiral and Commander-in-Chief of the German Navy. Dönitz was appointed by Hitler in the latter's last will and testament on 29 April 1945 as a last gesture of defiance during the last weeks of the Third Reich to even higher command. With both Göring and Himmler in disgrace and both men having been expelled from the Nazi Party and their State offices, Dönitz was appointed by Hitler to be his successor as Reichspräsident and Supreme Commander of the German Armed Forces.

110.
The German Navy: Naval Drum-Major, Speerwaffen-Obermech. Maat, 1937, The Uniform Jacket as Service Dress.

The Uniform Jacket was unique to the German Navy. It was worn both as part of the Service Dress and as a Summer Walking-out Uniform, when it was worn over either the blue or the white jumper with the blue collar worn outside the jacket. As it was an elaborate item of dress which served no practical function it was one of the naval garments that ceased to be issued at the outbreak of war and only those persons who already possessed the jacket could continue to use it within the prescribed circumstances.

111.
German Navy: Kapitän zur See, 1939, Formal Frock Coat Uniform.

The frock coat was an item of naval uniform prescribed for wear before the war by all naval officers including Administration officials. It was classed as Full Dress when worn together with epaulettes, the black felt cocked hat and the gold braided trousers. Medals were worn and the naval officers sword was carried. All accessories to the frock coat were in gilt for active naval officers and in silver for Marinebeamten. (see also Fig. 113).

112.
German Navy: Obermaat, 1943, Pea Jacket.

Seamen and Petty Officers in the German Navy were not issued with a greatcoat, instead they received a coat referred to as a 'Pea Jacket' made from thick navy-blue melton cloth. This was designed to be worn over the Uniform Jacket (Fig. 110) or the regulation jumpers (Fig. 117) with their collar worn inside the jacket. Collar patches worn on this jacket were in cornflower blue cloth with one horizontal strip of gold braid for the rank of Maat and two strips for Obermaat (Fig. 112).

113.
German Navy: Korvettenkapitän, 1939, Frock Coat as Formal Dress.

When the German naval frock coat was worn not with epaulettes (see Fig. 111) but with shoulder straps its use was prescribed for Formal Uniform, Formal Undress Uniform, Service Dress and Walking-out Dress. As Formal Dress the frock coat was worn with the naval officers peaked cap (here shown with a white cap cover for use during the summer months), white winged collar and black bow tie, full set of medals, parade belt and naval dagger. This item ceased to be used at the outbreak of war.

114.
German Navy: Stabsgefreiter, 1938, Shore Parade Dress.

The Shore Parade Dress was worn as its name implies by seamen and petty officers when ashore and when on parade or guard duty. The white version was worn during the summer months and consisted of a white jumper with a blue collar, blue cuffs and a black 'silk'. The melton cloth, navy blue trousers were worn outside the marching boots rolled up just above the ankles. The black leather waist belt on to which were fitted a pair of black leather rifle ammunition pouches were normally worn without the customary support of the leather 'Y' strap.

115.
German Navy: U-Boat Engine-Room Artificer, 1939, Protective Leather Clothing.

Protective leather clothing was provided for crews of

German submarines (U-Boats). They consisted of a pair of leather trousers and a leather jacket. There were two patterns of jacket. For use by engine-room crew members there was a short length jacket with a 'patrol neck' collar (Fig. 115), and for other crew members such as watch officers, the U-Boat commander, gun-teams etc. there was a three-quarter length coat with a large collar and large side pockets (not illustrated). Because of its short length the first type of jacket ensured that it was unlikely to become caught up in moving machinery; the second type afforded a certain degree of protection to its wearer when on deck in cold, wet or windy weather. The suits were produced in both black as well as grey-green coloured leather. They were meant to be used only for work on board the boat. When not in use they were kept stowed away on board. The ubiquitous Iron Cross Second Class shown here in Fig. 115 was not normally worn in this fashion other than at the time of its being awarded, as is the case in this illustration. Once awarded the decoration was acknowledged by the use of a small piece of the Iron Cross ribbon either worn through the button hole or worn mounted on a ribbon bar; instances of this are to be found in the colour plates of this book.

116.
German Navy: Naval Administration Official, Amtsrat technischer Beamte, 1941, Blue Reefer Jacket.

German Naval administration personnel, known as Marinebeamten, were officials employed by the Kriegsmarine to work as naval administrators within various shore-based departments and offices. Although they wore the same basic naval uniforms as the officers of the active navy they were distinguished from the navy proper by the use of silver coloured insignia, buttons and cap cords worn in place of the normal gold coloured insignia, buttons and black chin straps found on the uniforms and headdress of commissioned naval officers (Fig. 119).

117.
German Navy: Matrose, 1938, Navy-Blue Rig.

The Ordinary Seaman illustrated here is wearing what was the most frequently encountered uniform in the German Navy. Worn by Petty Officers and ratings alike it consisted of a navy-blue Melton cloth jumper and trousers to match. It had a mid-blue collar with an edging design of three white stripes and this was worn together with a black 'silk'. The five pointed gold star cloth badge worn on the left upper sleeve indicates the seaman's rating, that of Ordinary Seaman.

118.
German Navy: U-Boat Commander, Kapitänleutnant Lemp, U-30, 1940. Adapted British Army Battle Dress.

At the time of the fall of France large quantities of undamaged stocks of British Army clothing fell into German hands. Amongst these captured stores were quantities of British Army Battle Dress. In order to make full use of what would otherwise have been useless items the Germans issued these Battle Dress blouses and trousers to members of their U-Boat crews. It was felt that they would be able to make full use of these garments as work clothes without the risk of being mistaken for British troops. The uniforms were adapted with the use of German Naval buttons as well as naval shoulder straps being used. It was evident that these items were a popular form of work dress because when the original stocks of captured clothing became exhausted new work uniforms for U-Boat crews were manufactured by the Germans in a grey-green herringbone drill in almost the identical pattern to that of the British Army Battle Dress. It was an accepted practice that when at sea the white cloth cover worn on the naval officers peaked cap was always worn by the commander of the U-Boat and by no one else within the crew.

119.
German Navy: Kapitän zur See Freymadel, 1945, Naval Officers Blue Reefer Jacket.

The rank of an active naval officer was displayed on the blue reefer jacket by the use of sleeve rings and on the officers peaked cap by the use of a gold embroidered oak-leaf design. The reefer jacket was intended for use by officers when on parades ashore, as an Undress Uniform and for Walking-out dress.

120.
German Navy: Marine Unterhelferin, 1944, Regulation Female Top Coat.

Just as with the other branches of the Armed Forces, Women Auxiliary members were employed in the German Navy to undertake a whole range of office and clerical duties. Depicted here is a 'Marinehelferin' wearing the regulation grey top coat together with the navy blue side cap. The insignia worn above the cuff-title indicated that by trade she is a 'Writer'.

121, 122, 123.
German Navy Coastal Artillery. 121) Adjutant, 1943, Naval Tropical Uniform. 122) Matrose, 1944, Field Service Uniform. 123) Admiral of land based naval troops, 1944, Service Uniform.

German naval personnel operating and servicing shore based marine artillery batteries as well as junior ratings undergoing training at shore establishments wore a field-grey uniform. Although it was very similar in general design to the field-grey uniform worn throughout the German Army there were distinctive points which set it apart. The most obvious of these was the use of gold coloured buttons embossed with a fouled anchor design, gold national emblem and gilt shoulder strap braiding – also used around the collar by NCO ranks. The tunics as worn by the Marine Artillery personnel did not have the army type dark blue-green collar but instead the collar matched the field-grey of the uniform. The pockets on the skirt of the tunics were not of the patch type found on the Army tunics. The backing cloth to the national emblem, used as a backing to the 'Litzen' of the collar patches and as the cloth used on the basic shoulder straps for Men and NCO's was in dark bottle green (Fig. 122).

Tropical uniforms issued in a tan brown hue were standard issue to Marine Artillery units serving in hot climate countries (Fig. 121). Towards the last years of the war Admirals serving with shore based marine artillery units began to wear field-grey uniforms with Army pattern rank insignia in gold coloured embroidery on a cornflower blue backing (Fig. 123).

124, 125, 126.
German Air Sports Associations: 124) Fliegerkommandant 1935, Service Dress. 125) Aerodrome Supervisory Control Flugmeister 1935, Service Dress. 126) Flieger, 1933, Service Dress.

The DLV or German Air Sports Association was the forerunner of the Luftwaffe. Many aspects of its uniforms were similar to the uniforms introduced into the Luftwaffe from 1935. Both formations used the same basic blue-grey uniform colouring. Both had collar patch rank insignia of a similar basic design. The DLV collar patches were in four colours: white, black, yellow and blue which were four of the colours used by the Luftwaffe to distinguish certain of their personnel grades and branches. The Reichsluftaufsicht or Aerodrome Supervisory Control service used bright green as their distinguishing colour. Members of this organisation were responsible for controlling and observing the take-offs and landing of aircraft from airfields and aerodromes together with noting the performance and duration of individual flights. When on duty they wore a special gorget (Fig. 125).

127, 128.

German Air Force: Reichsmarschall des Grossdeutschen Reiches Hermann Göring, 1941, 1943.

Hermann Wilhelm Göring was the second most powerful personality in the National Socialist Movement. Born at Rosenheim in Bavaria on 12 January 1893 he was the son of a former governor of one of the German colonies in Africa. He was trained for service in the German Army and in 1912 he became a Lieutenant in the Infantry. He fought throughout the First World War first in the infantry, later with the German Air Arm. He had an exceptionally fine war record, being awarded the Iron Cross 1st Class and Imperial Germany's highest decoration for bravery the Pour le Mérite – the 'Blue Max'. In the last months of the war he commanded Geschwader Nr. 1 the famous Richthofen Squadron. He left Germany after the war was over and in 1921 he returned from living in Sweden where he had met and married his first wife Karin von Fock-Kantzow, and settled in Munich. It was here that he first heard and met with Hitler. He joined the Nazi Party in November 1922 and two months later took over the command of the SA (Storm Troops) from its first commander Johann Ulrich Klintsch. Göring took part in the abortive Munich Putsch of 9 November 1923 during which he suffered a dangerous wound which almost cost him his life. With help from his wife and friends he managed to flee to the Tyrol and later to Italy. He was eventually able to return to Germany under the amnesty of 1927.

On his return to Germany Göring became one of the first twelve National Socialist Deputies to enter the Reichstag (German Parliament). He was appointed President of the Reichstag on 30 August 1932 and after the Nazi 'Seizure of

Power' on 30 January 1933 he became Minister-President of Prussia. He was also appointed Commander-in-Chief of Prussian Police and he was both the founder and head of the Gestapo, the State Secret Police, an appointment which, together with control over concentration camps, he relinquished to Himmler on 1 April 1934. In March 1933 Göring founded the Deutsches Luftsports Verband, the DLV or German Air Sports Association, the forerunner of the Luftwaffe (Figs 124, 125, 126). On 28 April 1933 he founded and was head of the Reich Air Defence League-Reichsluftschutzbund-RLB-see colour plates (Figs 196, 197, 198). Five days later on 5 May he took on the appointment of Reich Minister for Aviation when the Reichskommissariat for Air, which he had headed since January 1933, was upgraded to a ministry. On 31 August 1933, Göring, who held the First World War Air Arm rank of Captain, was created a General of Infantry in the German Army by President Field Marshal von Hindenburg. Göring also held the SS Honorary rank of SS-Obergruppenführer, bestowed on him by Reichsführer-SS Heinrich Himmler. In April 1935 Hermann Göring now a widower married Emmy Sonnermann, his first wife Karin having died in Sweden in October 1931. On 26 February 1935 he became Commander-in-Chief of the newly constituted German Air Force with the rank of Luftwaffe General.

On the 20 April 1936 Hitler promoted Göring to Luftwaffe Generaloberst (Colonel General). In the same year Göring became Chief Forester and Hunting Master of the German Reich (Figs 220, 221, 222) and in September 1936 he was appointed Plenipotentiary for the Four-Year Plan. He was also Chairman of the Council of Ministers for the Defence of the Reich and head of the 'Reichswerke Hermann Göring'. On 28 April 1938 Göring was once again promoted by Hitler from Generaloberst to Generalfeldmarshall. On the outbreak of war on 1 September 1939 Hitler appointed Göring as his successor and after the fall of France on 19 July 1940 Göring was yet again promoted this time being elevated to the newly created and extraordinary rank of 'Reichsmarshall des Grossdeutschen Reiches' (Řeich Marshal of the Greater German Empirè).

In a nation that was besotted with the wearing of military and para-military uniforms of all kinds Göring stood out from all others in his love of uniformed attire. To distinguish his elevation to the rank of Reichsmarshall, Göring had a new uniform designed and tailored for himself in dove-grey material, the like of which had no equal within the German Armed Forces or the uniformed organisations of the Reich (Figs 127 & 128). Göring possessed at least six known versions of his Reich Marshal's jacket, all made from dove-grey materials but each with variations in cut and number of buttons, some of which were worn closed at the neck, others open to reveal white lapels. He had two versions of a top coat, the full-length greatcoat (Fig. 128) and a short three-quarter length version (not illustrated here: see Mollo/McGregor *Naval, Marine and Air Force Uniforms of World War 2*, Plate 18, Fig. 53). In addition to these he also wore a special cloak in a material matching his Reich Marshal's uniform. He possessed two forms of Reich Marshal peaked caps both illustrated here. Fig. 127 shows the less elaborate of the two and Fig. 128 has gold coloured laurel leaves embroidered into the material around the whole of the cap band. The collar patches shown in Fig. 127 were the second pattern Reichsmarshall patches. The original set featured a Wehrmacht eagle (right patch) and crossed batons (left patch) both within a surround of gold embroidered laurel leaves and all worked on to a base of white velvet. These were not to Göring's liking. In March 1941 he had a second type made which are featured here and show both patches with crossed Marshal's batons. In Fig. 127 Göring is shown carrying his Interim-Stab and in Fig. 128 he is saluting with his Marshal's baton.

129.

German Air Force: Former Reichsmarshall Hermann Göring, 1945.

In April 1945 Hermann Göring fell completely from grace. He was expelled by Hitler from the National Socialist Party. He was stripped of his rank of Reich Marshal and he was dismissed from his post as Commander-in-Chief of the Luftwaffe. Hitler, living out his last remaining days in his Berlin bunker, had Göring placed under arrest by the SS. In contravention of his 1 September 1939 decree, and before committing suicide, Hitler chose Grand Admiral Dönitz (Fig. 109) to be his successor and not Göring. With Hitler dead Göring, together with his family and members of his close staff, all of whom had been under SS arrest at Obersalzberg, managed to escape being shot by the SS and made their way towards the advancing American Forces in order to give themselves up. On 9 May 1945 at Kitzbühel in Austria Göring surrendered to First Lieutenant Jerome N. Shapiro the first American soldier he encountered and an officer from the US 36th Infantry Division under the command of Brigadier-General Robert J. Stack.

A few days later Göring, accompanied by his Aide, Oberst Berndt von Brauschitsch, entered a detention camp at Augsberg dressed in yet another style of uniform that differed from any other he possessed (Fig. 129). He carried his Reich Marshal's baton inside its cloth cover. The jewelled encrusted decoration he wore, along with his favourite hunting dagger, his gold wrist watch, rings, pens, cigar cases, pill boxes and his many other personel effects were all taken from him. In the case of his decoration they were broken up for the value of their precious stones and metals.

130.

German Air Force: Lieutenant of Air Signals, 1938, Officers Formal Evening Full Dress.

The German Air Force shared with the German Navy and

the German Diplomatic Corps (Fig. 188) the distinction of being the only uniformed organisations of the Third Reich that provided for Evening Full Dress to be worn by its officer classes. The Luftwaffe possessed two versions of their Evening Full Dress, the Formal Evening Full Dress and the Informal Evening Full Dress. The former, which is illustrated here (Fig. 130) differed from the latter in that it was worn with aiguillettes (silver for officers, gilt for Generals and above), white bow tie, white waistcoat and full sets of medals. The informal version had a black bow tie, blue-grey waistcoat of the same coloured material as the Full Dress itself and only ribbons mounted on a ribbon bar were worn. Black shoes were worn as were white gloves. No hat was worn with this uniform.

131.
German Air Force: Generaloberst, 1938, Air Force Service Tunic worn as Parade Dress.

The four pocket, open neck Service Tunic or 'Tuchrock' was an item of Luftwaffe dress worn by all ranks of the Air Force. Its use was widespread and until the introduction on 11 November 1938 of the Uniform Tunic or Luftwaffe 'Waffenrock' (Fig. 134), it was worn on the following occasions.

As a Parade Dress by certain grades of Warrant Officers, by all officers and by Generals (as shown here in Fig. 131). When worn with a blue-grey shirt and black tie it was used as Service Dress, Undress and Reporting Uniform by all officers. It was permitted to be used for both Walking-out (white shirt and black tie) and for Flying Service when it replaced the use of the Flight Blouse (blue-grey shirt and black tie) (Fig. 135). It was also used as both Formal and Informal Full Dress for day-time use by officers, worn together with white shirt, stiff collar and black tie, or Formal and Informal Full Dress for NCOs and Men also worn with white shirt, stiff collar and black tie.

132.

German Air Force: Air Force Administration Official with the rank of General, 1940. The Special Tunic 'Kleiner Rock' for Generals and above.

Air Force officers from the rank of General upwards including Administrative Officials and Air Force Engineers of General's rank had as part of their military wardrobe a special tunic, referred to as the 'Kleiner Rock' or Little Coat, that could be worn as Walking-out Dress, Undress and Informal Full Dress. It was always worn together with the officers' broad striped, long trousers. The distinctive feature of this tunic was the use of wide coloured lapel facings and piping down the front of the tunic and around the tops of the turn-back cuffs. Air Force Generals were distinguished by white facings and piping, whilst Engineer Officers displayed Rose pink facings and piping. The broad stripes on their trousers matched the colour used on the tunics. Air Force Administration Officials permitted to wear this tunic had, before February 1940, worn dark green facings and piping together with broad dark green trouser stripes. This however was altered after 16 February so that white trouser stripes were introduced (Fig. 132) and were worn together with the dark green facing and piping of the tunic. Production of these tunics ceased at the outbreak of war but those officers who already possessed such a tunic were permitted to continue to wear it.

133.

German Air Force: Feldwebel, Regiment General Göring, 1938, NCO's Summer Walking-out Dress.

Unlike the Army the German Air Force provided, before the war, a summer uniform, – blue-grey Service Tunic and white trousers – for its Men and NCOs and an all white summer uniform of white tunic and trousers for wear by its officers and officials of all ranks. This practice ceased after

1939 and only those persons who possessed such items were permitted to continue using them. As a form of summer dress these items of apparel were to have been used from 1 April to the 30 September each year, weather permitting. The white top summer cap had a cloth top that was removable.

134.
German Air Force: Stabswachtmeister, Horst Wessel Squadron, 1940. The Uniform Tunic.

The Waffenrock or Uniform Tunic first introduced into the Luftwaffe in November 1938 was intended to replace the two earlier Air Force uniforms, the Service Tunic (Tuchrock) (Figs 131, 133) and the Flight Blouse (Fliegerbluse) (Fig. 135). In its general appearance it was very similar to the Service Tunic but the Uniform Tunic was cut in such a way that, by the addition of an extra button, the tunic could be worn buttoned at the neck. All other features remained the same. Although the actual rank of this Artillery NCO is that of Oberwachtmeister he wears the double sleeve rings indicating that he holds the appointment of Hauptwacht-meister. The cuff title is that for Zerstörer Geschwader 26 'Horst Wessel' and the yellow duty cords worn around the right shoulder indicate he is duty NCO for that day.

135.
German Air Force: Fighter Squadron Hauptmann, 1945, Flight Service Blouse.

The Flight Blouse or 'Fliegerbluse' was the Air Force equivalent of the jacket worn with the Army's Special Panzer Uniform (Fig. 93). It was especially designed for use by flying personnel on the same principle in that it allowed for ease of movement when worn by a pilot in the close confines of an aircraft cockpit. There was no 'skirt' to the single breasted blouse, no cuffs or attached belt; it was fly-fronted with no external buttons and in certain cases had only two small pockets. It proved an ideal garment for its purpose. As with all the standard items of Luftwaffe dress this flight blouse was available for use by all ranks, it being an item of issue to NCOs and Men and was purchased by officers of all ranks including Generals and Administration Officials, usually made from better quality material. Flight blouses produced before the war were for Men and NCOs without external pockets and up to 1 October 1940 they had no Luftwaffe National Emblem on the right breast. On 19 November 1940 two side pockets with an external button to each pocket flap were added and after 1 October 1940 the basic Luftwaffe National Emblem was displayed. Officers on the other hand had always worn the Luftwaffe National Emblem and they initially had side pockets with curved flapless openings. Flaps to these pockets were introduced from November 1940. The Fliegerbluse when worn by NCOs and Men open at the neck was worn with the regulation blue-grey neck band and by officers with the blue-grey shirt and black tie. Although originally intended for use when flying the appearance of this item proved to be smart enough and its use convenient and popular enough for it to be worn throughout the Luftwaffe by all branches. The Flight Blouse along with the Tuchrock (Fig. 133, Fig. 131) was intended to be replaced after November 1938 by the Waffenrock (Fig. 134) but this was not done and all three items continued in use right up to the end of the war.

136, 137, 138.
German Air Force: 136) Oberfeldwebel, Fighter Pilot, 1944, 'Invasion Suit'. 137) Aircrew member Fähnrich, 1939, 'Bulgarian Suit'. 138) Bomber Pilot Feldwebel, 1940, Summer Flying Suit.

The German Air Force provided a variety of special protective flight clothing to be worn by its air crews. Initially these were of three types.

1) The lightweight tan coloured summer flying suit for flights over all types of terrain (Fig. 138). This was worn over the normal Flight Blouse or Service Tunic worn together with either officers breeches or trousers. The unlined flight helmet was made from the same lightweight tan material. The bright yellow cover worn over the helmet was introduced in an effort to make the wearer more conspicuous in the event of his having to bale out of his aircraft and ditch into the sea. The kapok filled life jacket was of the type normally worn by bomber crews and crews of transport and flying medical units. Passengers in transport aircraft would also wear this type of life jacket. The heavy duty leather and suede fleece lined boots were standard issue to pilots and air crews of all types of aircraft.

2) The heavyweight fleece-lined flying suit for use during winter months when flying over land (Fig. 137).

Although the flying suit depicted here (Fig. 137) is a dark blue-grey garment it was also manufactured in dark brown and dark-grey material. It was sometimes referred to as the 'Bulgarian Suit'. The life jacket is the inflatable type normally worn by fighter pilots and those whose movement was restricted inside a single seat cockpit and where the bulkier kapok filled jackets would prove too cumbersome. The Airman is wearing the Luftwaffe Fliegermütze, the 'fore and aft' flight hat.

3) The two-piece fleece-lined leather flying suit for winter flights over sea areas (not illustrated). As the war progressed it became evident to the German Air Force authorities that a more practical form of flying apparel was needed. Pilots of fighter aircraft had for some time taken to wearing flying jerkins made from cloth and leather. These were very popular and much easier to put on and take off than a complete flying suit and as a development of these jerkins a new form of flying outfit was introduced into Air Force service. Sometimes known as the 'Invasion Suit' (Fig. 136), because its initial and widespread use happened to coincide

with the Allied Invasion of the Normandy coast, it consisted of a cloth jerkin with matching trousers in blue-grey material. These trousers were very distinctive with their large map pockets. The Oberfeldwebel depicted here is shown wearing the Luftwaffe Replacement Model 1943 cap, an item of soft headdress that was intended to replace the Fliegermütze. The practice of attaching a small belt of flare pistol cartridges around the pilot's calf was something individual airmen chose to do. There were no laid down regulations that said this had to be done in this manner and although it may have ensured that a pilot in distress had a plentiful and ready supply of cartridges to hand he ran the risk of death or mutilation if these cartridges were hit by gunfire or he had been trapped by the legs inside his burning aircraft.

139.
German Air Force: Leutnant, Panzer-Division 'Hermann Göring', 1943. Special Black Panzer Uniform.

The 'Hermann Göring' Brigade was formed in the summer of 1942 from Regiment 'General Göring' and in January 1943 it was converted into a Panzer Division. As early as 1938 when Regiment 'General Göring' was first formed the members of its Panzer Reconnaissance Unit wore the Special Black Panzer Uniform. This practice was continued throughout the development of the formation by all those manning enclosed armoured vehicles. The uniform was identical in design to those used by Army (Fig. 93), Waffen-SS (Fig. 154) and Police Panzer Units (Fig. 180). The Luftwaffe version was only distinguished from the uniforms of other armoured forces by the use of Air Force insignia. This consisted of the Luftwaffe National Emblem worn on the right breast, the 'Hermann Göring' cuff-title on the right cuff and the use of white Waffenfarbe piping to the collar and death's head collar patches.

140.
German Air Force: Capitán, Flying Branch, Legion Condor, 1939, Parade Uniform.

In July 1936 a nationalist revolt, led by General Franco and General Mola, broke out against the Spanish Republic. Starting first in the military garrisons of Spanish Morocco it rapidly spread to the Spanish mainland. Within days of this happening Hitler began to send detachments of 'Volunteers' from Germany to Spain to support Franco in what Hitler saw as the Spanish Generals' 'fight against Bolshevism'. These volunteers were detached from the regular Air Force units stationed in Germany and sent secretly to Spain. Flying personnel and ground crews were sent with troops from anti-aircraft units as well as medical and signals troops together with administration personnel. The German Army also had a small contingent of volunteers serving in Spain, mostly with the Spanish Nationalist tank forces. German Naval units saw action in Spanish waters. The Legion Condor – the name given to this body of German Volunteers, a large percentage of which were German Air Force personnel – was initially a volunteer force. Its status however was changed once the value of the battle experience gained by these troops began to show results. The volunteer system was scrapped and for the rest of the war a regular supply of German officers and men were rotated from Germany to Spain and back at six to ten months intervals. At the successful completion of the war in April 1939 the German personnel serving in Spain were returned to Germany and after a number of official parades held in both Hamburg and Berlin together with awards being presented to all who had participated in the Spanish Civil War the Legion Condor was officially disbanded.

Illustrated here is an officer holding the Legion rank of Capitán as indicated by the three, six-pointed silver stars worn on his tunic and cap. The backing to these stars (and NCO's bars) was in a coloured cloth indicating the branch of

169

service of the wearer, in this case yellow for flight personnel. The officer also wears his Spanish Air Force pilots wings above his right breast pocket and the 'Spanish Cross', a German award for service in the Legion, on his right breast pocket. When the Legion returned home to Germany it was realised that the troops were deficient in a universally coloured uniform of a standard pattern. Prior to the 'Homecoming' parade taking place in Berlin a mad rush ensued to find suitable uniforms of the right colour and in sufficient numbers for the contingent to wear. Eventually a stock of Reichs Arbeitsdienst uniforms (see Figs 70 to 74) was located and all the tailors within the Berlin area were put to work in converting these RAD tunics into uniforms for the Legion Condor.

141.
German Air Force: Fl.-Generalstabsingenieur, 1940, Greatcoat as Parade Dress.

The pre-war structure of the Luftwaffe was divided into four main branches: a) The active regular formations which included both ground forces and flying units, b) the Administrative officials, c) The Corps of Navigational Experts and d) The Corps of Engineers. This last formation was identified by a branch colour of rose pink. The colour was used for the corps collar patches, as underlays on shoulder straps and as lapel facings to the greatcoat of its two most senior General officer ranks. As with all Air Force Officers of General's rank those engineers who held the equivalent rank of general were distinguished by the use of gilt insignia, piping and buttons. The rank of Leading Flight Chief Engineer was changed in 1940 to that of Flight General Staff Engineer.

142, 144.
German Air Force: 142) Hauptmann, 1942, Tropical Clothing. 144) German Air Force Paratroop: Jäger, 1941, Tropical Clothing.

German Luftwaffe personnel, including paratroopers, were issued with a set of tan coloured Tropical Clothing which was authorised to be worn between 1 May and 30 September, weather permitting, within the boundaries of the Reich. When the same clothing was worn in North Africa it was permitted to be worn throughout the year. It consisted of a tunic (Fig. 142) and or shirt (Fig. 144), long trousers (Fig. 142) or shorts worn with the tropical forage cap, the tropical service cap (Fig. 142) or sun helmet (similar to sun helmet in Fig. 100). Footwear consisted of lace-up boots (Fig. 142) or lace-up shoes. The shirt worn without the tunic, the shorts and the sun helmet were not, however, allowed to be worn within the home area.

In other hot climate areas or countries such as Italy (south of the Naples-Foggia line), Sicily, Sardinia, Greece, Crete and Rhodes and other Mediterranean islands under German control the clothing was worn between the dates 1 May and 30 September. The Tropical Service Cap (Fig. 142) was introduced for wear with the Luftwaffe tan coloured uniform on 13 April 1942. It took the place of the Tropical Forage Cap and was worn by Men, NCOs and Officers. It tended to be worn fairly extensively by members of the Hermann Göring Division when serving in North Africa, Tunisia, Sicily and Italy. They gave it the name of the 'Hermann Meyer Cap', a witticism reflecting Hermann Göring's unofficial name. The 'Afrika' cuff-title with the silver-white lettering on a dark blue cloth band was a Luftwaffe cuff-title worn only by Air Force personnel actually stationed in North Africa. The Captain shown in Fig. 142 had at one time served in the Legion Condor during the Spanish Civil War of 1936-39 (see Fig. 140). He is wearing the Spanish Cross with swords in silver worn on the right breast below the Spanish Air Force pilots 'wings'.

171

143.
German Air Force Paratroops: Oberjäger, 1943, Special Protective Parachute clothing and Jump Harness.

The Special Parachute Protective Clothing issued to German paratroop personnel underwent a number of changes during the existence of the German Parachute Arm. Originally paratroopers had been issued with a plain grey-green jump smock known as a 'Bone Bag' that whilst it opened at the front was a step-in type of garment with two short 'legs'. The second pattern smock, made from printed camouflage material (Fig. 143) opened all the way down the front, a much more practical item of wear. Fabric covered rubber knee pads were issued to troops undergoing training. These were intended to protect the wearers' knees on landing from a jump. Leather gloves with extended wrist covering were part of this specialist clothing. The rimless steel helmet with its leather chin strap securely anchored in three places was designed to afford maximum head protection without being cumbersome and at the same time fit securely without the risk of the helmet being thrown off the wearer's head on impact with the ground. The parachute harness shown in Fig. 143 was the final pattern issued to Paratroopers. It should not be confused with the parachute harness as worn by Luftwaffe Air Crews. Jump boots in black or dark brown leather were originally side lace-up (Fig. 144) but later were replaced by less expensive front lace-up ankle boots (Fig. 143).

145.
German Air Force: Gefreiter Brigade Hermann Göring, 1942, Camouflage smock and Field Service Uniform.

The troops of the Brigade 'Hermann Göring' first began to be issued with camouflage smocks and helmet covers from stocks of Waffen-SS camouflage items in July 1942. Not all members of the Brigade received these garments as there were not enough smocks and helmet covers to go around. A year after the first issues of these Waffen-SS patterned items had been made, additional camouflage clothing of the standard Army 'splinter' pattern (see Fig. 103) began to be issued, followed later by the 'tan, water pattern' type.

146.
German Air Force: Major, Parachute Regiment, 1944, Officers Leather overcoat.

The Leather Overcoat was an item of clothing that was obtained by the individual officer at his own expense. Many officers of all services favoured wearing the Leather Overcoat, the basic design was universal and only the shade of colour changed for some of the more obvious service branches ie: grey-green for Army and Waffen-SS officers, blue-grey for Air Force and Paratroop officers, as is the case illustrated here, dark blue-grey for naval officers etc. The only insignia permitted to be worn on these coats were shoulder straps.

147.
German Air Force: Grenadier, Luftwaffe Field Division, 1944 Air Force Field Division combat jacket.

In the autumn of 1942 efforts were made to put new life into the dwindling forces of the German Army fighting on the Eastern Front by drawing on the excessive manpower available in both the Navy and the Air Force. On Göring's insistence the surplus men taken from his Air Force units were formed into ground-combat Field Divisions under Luftwaffe control. The 'combing out' process from Luftwaffe ground units, anti-aircraft units and recruit depots produced in all some twenty Luftwaffe Field Divisions together with the requisite replacement and training units. Most of the divisions were sent to the Russian Front during the winter of 1942-43 whilst some fought in Italy and others in France in 1944. In the autumn of 1943 the Luftwaffe Field Divisions were absorbed into the Army, many of them having suffered heavy losses and a number of the badly mauled divisions were disbanded altogether. Although initially fitted out with Luftwaffe uniforms and personal equipment the divisions were forced by circumstances to adapt their clothing to suit their needs. Hence the introduction of a camouflage combat jacket (Fig. 147) which was unique to the Field Divisions, and the use of field-grey clothing when Luftwaffe blue-grey was no longer suitable or available. They did however continue to display the Luftwaffe National Emblem and they also wore special collar patches which were peculiar to the troops of these formations.

148, 150.
German Air Force Female Auxiliaries: 148) Flakwaffenhelferin, 1945, Service Uniform with Greatcoat. 150) Betriebs-Gruppenführerin und Heimleiterin, 1940, Duty Uniform.

Women were employed in the Luftwaffe in more capacities than in any other branch of German military or administrative work. Female auxiliaries in the German Air Force were engaged as telephone and telegraph operators, filing clerks, as radio operators, in the Air Warning Service, as plotting operators, intelligence service assistants, as searchlight crews, medical personnel and as flak-crew assistants. They wore uniforms of Luftwaffe blue-grey, some girls wore skirts but when this was not practical they wore slacks. Various systems existed at different times used to indicate auxiliary ranks, almost all were based on the use of flat silver braid worn either as bars or chevrons. These were arranged on the principle that the more chevrons or bars worn – the higher was the wearer's rank. Members of Flak units (Flakwaffenhelferinen) wore a distinctive shield-shaped cloth badge, displaying a Luftwaffe eagle and sword overlaying a

174

sword, and worn on the right upper arm of their tunics and greatcoats (Fig. 148). The yellow Service Lanyard (Fig. 150) was worn by Officers and NCOs when acting as Duty Officer or NCO for the day (see also Fig. 134).

149.
SS Female Auxiliary: SS-Assistent, 1944, Walking-out Uniform.

Women employed as office personnel in SS establishments should not be confused with those SS females who were responsible for the running of concentration camps for women prisoners. Although both categories of SS Women wore uniforms the example shown here in Fig. 149 is the type of SS Auxiliary in a strictly clerical capacity.

151, 152, 153.
Armed-SS: 151) SS-Brigadeführer und Generalmajor der Waffen-SS, 1940, Greatcoat, 152) SS-Untersturmführer, 1943, Walking-out Uniform, 153) SS-Sturmmann, Musician, 1944, Service Uniform.

Units of the SS-Special Purpose Troops that existed before the Polish campaign of 1939 were enlarged during the next eighteen months and new units brought into being. By April 1941 the original name of SS-Verfügungstruppe was officially changed to that of Waffen-SS or Armed-SS. The former earth grey clothing had been gradually replaced by uniforms of field-grey. Waffen-SS officers of the rank of SS-Oberführer and above wore greatcoats that had silver-grey lapel facings (Fig. 151). The army pattern service tunic, with both the dark blue-green collar (Fig. 152) and the plain field grey version (Fig. 153) were used extensively by all ranks of the Waffen-SS. The cuff-title was an item of insignia that was widely used throughout the many units of the SS, both the General-SS and Armed-SS, the latter having a vast number of types and qualities of manufacture for the cuff-titles used by so many of their named units.

154.
Armed-SS: 154) SS-Obersturmbannführer, 1944, Black Panzer Uniform.

The SS crews and replacement crews of enclosed armoured vehicles such as tanks, armoured cars and armoured radio vehicles were issued with the SS version of the special Black Panzer uniform. It was originally intended to be worn when serving with an armoured vehicle and when first brought into use by the SS in 1938 it was for this express purpose, in exactly the same way as the Army issued its armoured crews with their black Panzer uniform (Fig. 93). However, the uniform proved to be increasingly popular with the troops to the extent that it was worn on every suitable occasion.

155.
Armed-SS: SS-Obersturmführer, 1945, service Tunic and Tropical Shorts.

Although the Waffen-SS did not have any of its military units participating in the North African campaign members of the Waffen-SS saw service in southern Russia, the Crimea, Greece, Italy, Yugoslavia, the Mediterranean and southern France, all countries and areas subject to extreme heat during the summer months. Under these conditions the Waffen-SS troops were issued with tropical clothing. The SS-Obersturmführer shown here in Fig.155 is wearing a mixture of temperature climate service jacket, tailored to his own personal taste, with khaki drill shorts and the tropical version of the Model 1943 Replacement Field Cap.

156.
Armed-SS: SS-Untersturmführer, 1944, Field Grey special uniform for crews of self-propelled artillery and anti-tank units.

The Waffen-SS field-grey version of the special uniform

illustrated in Fig. 154 is shown here. It was basically the same pattern as worn in the Army (Fig. 101) but it was cut shorter at the waist and it had the obvious addition of Waffen-SS insignia.

This type of uniform made its first appearance when it was worn by the assault gun crews of the Leibstandarte SS 'Adolf Hitler' Division during the Balkan campaign of the summer of 1941. A year later in August 1942 its use was extended to crews of self-propelled artillery weapons and by December of that same year and for the duration it was being issued to crews of self-propelled anti-tank units. (Fig. 156).

157, 158, 159.
Armed SS: 157) SS-Unterscharführer, 1944, Camouflage Smock. 158) SS-Sturmmann, 1943, Camouflage Winter Uniform. 159) SS-Oberscharführer, 1943, Camouflage Field Uniform.

The Armed-SS (Waffen-SS) had made far more use of camouflage clothing and items of camouflage than any of the other fighting services. The Waffen-SS clothing authorities had produced a number of camouflage items of clothing in a variety of patterns and colours. The three figures featured here illustrate the basic patterns and colours used and show some of the items of clothing in use at different times. Fig. 157 shows the typical summer camouflage patterning on the Waffen-SS 'Tiger Jacket'. Fig. 158 features the autumn patterning used on the reversible Winter uniforms. These uniforms were of the same design as those used by the Army and to a lesser extent other ground fighting forces. They differed only in that they displayed the distinctive tan, brown and black ragged spot design. Fig. 159 shows a mixture of various SS camouflage patterns. The jacket is patterned with the summer 'foliage' design, the trousers have the final-pattern autumn colouring. The steel helmet has a cover made from Italian Army camouflage material.

160, 161, 162.
Armed-SS: 160) SS-Scharführer 1942, Snow camou-
flage cotton smock. 161) SS-Oberscharführer, 1941,
Greatcoat. 162) SS-Schütze, 1943, Fur-lined Anorak.

'General Winter' proved to be as formidable an enemy to the
German troops as did the Red Army itself. German units
fighting in Russia and on the Eastern Front during the first
winter of 1941–42 suffered very badly in the appalling
sub-zero temperatures. Frost bite and death by freezing
(hypothermia) added heavily to the losses inflicted on them
by the Russians. Warm winter clothing was absolutely
essential if German troops were to fight another winter
campaign. The Special Winter Uniform, already described in
Fig. 103 (Army) and Fig. 157 (Waffen-SS) was hurriedly
manufactured and rushed to the troops, mostly Army
troops, in time for the 1942–43 winter period. The Waffen-
SS produced their own version of the same garment (Fig.
157) and these too were distributed to their troops. The
winter clothing proved to be both practical and comfortable
so much so that those front line troops fortunate enough to
be issued with the uniform very soon wore it all the time,
fighting, sleeping and eating in the garments. As one side of
the uniform was in white to blend with the snow this very
quickly became filthy dirty, defeating the whole purpose of
snow white camouflage. These uniforms were impossible to
wash under front line conditions, the inter-lining being of a
wool-rayon mixture not very easy to dry out without the
right kind of machinery. Therefore in order to overcome this
problem simple white cotton smocks were made that were
worn over the special winter clothing and which, if they
became soiled, could easily be cleaned in or near the fighting
zones. The greatcoat, shown here in Fig. 161 proved
completely inadequate for the winter fighting on the Eastern
Front, and it was this type of cold weather garment that was
eventually replaced by the far more suitable fur-lined and
hooded water repellent, pull-on, winter anorak, Fig. 162.

163.

German Police Formations: Hauptwachtmeister der Verkehrspolizei, 1937, Parade Uniform.

The German Traffic Police consisted of specially trained units of men who were stationed alongside the Barracks Police in all major German cities. They were responsible for regulating the traffic and patrolling the main roads. They were well versed in the field of Traffic Law and were made responsible for the prevention of traffic accidents, the speedy assistance by traffic accident patrols at the scene of an accident and the piecing together and recording of the causes of such accidents. Because of the somewhat hazardous nature of their work these Traffic Police wore white linen jackets and long white cotton coats when on duty. Their insignia and buttons were gilt and they wore black breeches with black leather boots (Fig. 163).

164, 165.

German Police Formations: 164) Leutnant der Schutzpolizei des Reiches, 1939, Parade Uniform. 165) Wachtmeister der Schutzpolizei, 1938, Parade Uniform.

The uniform worn for pre-war and early wartime Police parades by members of the Schutzpolizei were those as illustrated here (Figs 164, 165). Officers wore the silver with black and red silk design brocade belt and cartouche pouch cross strap and silver aiguillettes. Other ranks wore the Police Shako with Parade Plume. This was in white horse hair for all officers, red plumes were worn by Police Musicians and black plumes were for all other police personnel (see Fig. 178).

166.

German Police Formations: Oberwachtmeister der Motorisierten Gendarmeriebereitschaft, 1935, Service Uniform.

After 1 April 1935 when the SA Feldjägerkorps ceased to

exist as a separate Party police force their members were absorbed into the Reich Protection Police. Special formations of Motorised Gendarmerie Emergency Units were organised charged with the task of patrolling the German State Autobahn systems. These Bereitschaften were made up in the initial stages from the members of the FJK. This fact can clearly be seen by the influence they had in the choice of white used as their facing colour, the retention of a gorget of almost identical pattern to that worn by the FJK as well as the overall colour of their uniform. These special Autobahn police had a short existence. Their task was eventually taken over by the Motorised Gendarmerie (Fig. 178) and the members of these units were absorbed into the regular Reich Protection Police completely losing any semblance of their former origins.

167.
German Police Formations: Oberwachtmeister der Marine-Küsten Polizei, 1940, Service Dress, Summer.

The uniform and certain items of insignia worn by members of the Naval Coastal Police detachments were initially the same as worn by the Waterways Protection Police (see Fig. 172). The insignia was later changed to regular naval pattern.

The gorget worn by these 'Coastguard' police personnel was one of the smallest of all the gorgets worn and it was different also in that instead of being suspended from around the wearer's neck by a 'chain', it was attached to the jacket or greatcoat by a long metal prong on the back of the gorget which was passed through two cotton loops stitched to the coat.

Members of the Coastal Police wore a narrow dark blue cuff-title edged yellow and with the yellow gothic lettering 'Marine-Küstenpolizei'.

168.

German Police Formations: Hauptwachtmeister der Schutzpolizei der Gendarmerie, 1941, Service Uniform.

The Gendarmerie or Rural Police was a branch of the Ordnungspolizei. In those communities of less than 2,000 inhabitants and in the open countryside, Order Police protection was afforded by the Gendarmerie. It also included the Motorised Traffic Gendarmerie (Fig. 178) and the Mountain Gendarmerie (Fig. 169).

The uniforms of the Gendarmerie personnel were distinguished from those worn by their opposite numbers in the Schutzpolizei. Gendarmerie used light brown leather trimming and equipment in all those parts of the uniform where the Schutzpolizei (see Figs 164, 165) used black. Cuffs and collars to Gendarmerie tunics were in light brown as compared to dark brown and their piping colour was orange as opposed to the green used by the Reich Protection Police.

169.

German Rural Police: Wachtmeister, Mountain Police, 1943, Service Uniform.

In those areas of the Reich, including the annexed territories, that were of a mountainous nature or were prone to heavy snow fall during the winter months specially trained members of the Gendarmerie, skilled in skiing and mountaineering, were employed. Members of the Mountain Gendarmerie (Hochgebirgs Gendarmerie) had to undergo a period of four years practical experience in mountaineering and rock climbing before qualifying as a specialist with the right to be known as an expert and entitled to wear the badge of an expert mountaineer.

Skiers in the Mountain Gendarmerie were similarly treated. Three schools existed before the war to teach the Mountain Gendarmerie the art of skiing. These were situated at

Oberjoch bei Hindelang, Sudelfeld am Wendelstein and at Kitzbühel in the Tirol.

The personnel of the Hochgebirgs Gendarmerie wore the same basic green uniform as worn by the Schutzploizei but were distinguished as Gendarmerie personnel by having light brown cuffs and collars to their tunics and greatcoats piped in orange piping. They wore long trousers tucked into mountaineering boots and also wore the Mountain Police Bergmütze (Mountain or ski cap) with police insignia in either cloth or metal. No Bezirk or area name appeared above the police eagle arm badge worn on the left sleeve of their tunics.

170.
German Order Police: SS-Obergruppenführer und General der Waffen-SS und Polizei Alfred Wünnenberg, 1942, Police General's Service Uniform.

Under the Weimar Republic there was no National Police Force in Germany. Each Land or State had its own police, the controlling authority being usually the Minister of the Interior of the Land. In January 1934, a year after coming to power, the Nazis began to reorganise the German Police by transferring the right to exercise police power from the Länder to the Reich. This process of centralisation culminated in the creation of the post of Chef der Deutschen Polizei im Reichsministerium des Innern (Chief of the German Police in the Reich Ministry of the Interior). Himmler (Fig. 41), shortly after his appointment to this office, divided the German police into two main departments: the Sicherheitspolizei (Security Police or SIPO) and the Ordnungspolizei (Order Police or Uniformed Police, ORPO).

From its inception to the summer of 1943 command of the Ordnungspolizei was held by General der Polizei und Chef der Ordnungspolizei Kurt Daluege. He was succeeded from 1943 to 1945 by SS-Obergruppenführer und General der

Waffen-SS und Polizei Alfred Wünnenberg. Fig. 170 shows Wünnenberg at the time he commanded the SS-Polizei-Division. He wears a mixture of Army and Police uniform items, Army tunic with National Emblem worn on the left sleeve together with Police General's cap badge, collar patches and shoulder straps.

171.
German Police Formations: Feuerschutzpolizei Revieroberwachtmeister, 1938, Fire Fighting Uniform.

Although Prussia had incorporated its fire-fighting organisations into the Police system in 1933, this amalgamation was only made universal throughout the Reich in 1938. In view of the necessity for air-raid protection about ninety of the larger German cities were ordered to transfer their existing fire-fighting personnel to the newly created Fire Protection Police. The Feuerschutzpolizei was a branch of the Ordnungspolizei and as such came under the command of the same higher police authorities which controlled the latter. The age limit for the Fire Protection Police was sixty years. The officers had to have been graduates of the Fire Protection Officers School at Eberswald.

The smallest administrative area was the Wachtbezirk composed usually of several ordinary Schutzpolizei Reviere (Wards). Operational areas for actual fire-fighting were determined independently, however, and Ausrückbereiche (operational zones) were drawn in conformity with tactical considerations. The usual operational unit called out in the first instance was known as a Zug, and the corresponding Feuerschutzpolizei Wache was known as a Zugwache (Watch Squad). In exceptional cases a larger unit, the Gruppe, was called out and the corresponding Wache was known as a Gruppenwache (Watch Group). The commander in charge of the local units of the Feuerschutzpolizei was called Kommandeur or Leiter. He directed fire-fighting and fire prevention, allotted the respective zones of operation to the subordinate units, and generally supervised the organisation and operation of the Feuerschutzpolizei under his command. He was responsible for administrative purposes to the Oberbürgermeister or Bürgermeister. The size of the Fire Protection Police was fixed in accordance with the population of the city; but in those cities with more than 870,000 inhabitants and in those with harbour installations, numerous industrial or large areas which presented particular fire hazards, the number and the nature of the Feuerschutzpolizei Wachen was determined in each case individually.

In cities with more than 150,000 population, auxiliary fire-fighting units called Freiwillige Feuerwehren were established on a voluntary basis to supplement the Feuerschutzpolizei. They were organised into tactical units called Gruppen. In exceptional cases, where the Freiwillige Feuerwehr was inadequate, an obligatory fire service, the Pflichtfeuerwehr, was established.

Both the Fire Protection Police (Feuerschutzpolizei) and the Volunteer Fire Defence Service (Freiwillige Feuerwehr) wore identical blue-black (Prussian blue) uniforms with black facings and carmine pink piping and insignia. Only the collar patches differed and the inner colour of their shoulder straps distinguished between the two formations.

Upon absorbtion into the Order Police, the Fire Protection Police wore the police eagle arm badge in carmine pink with the name of their Bezirk or district above on the left upper arm of their tunics, work overalls and greatcoats. From 1938 the Fire Protection Police began to be issued with uniforms of police-green material with black cuffs and collars, piped crimson. These facings were later changed to brown when all police uniforms began to be standardized from September 1942. The Prussian blue Fire Police uniforms continued in use throughout the war right up to the capitulation. The Fire Police helmet was produced both with and without the polished metal 'comb'. The helmet's leather neck flap was detachable.

172.
Reich Protection Police: Waterways Protection Police Wachtmeister, 1941. Greatcoat.

The Waterways Protection Police (Wasserschutzpolizei) was a branch of the Schutzpolizei responsible for policing and patrolling all navigable inland rivers and canals, regulating waterborne traffic, preventing smuggling, enforcing safety and security measures and inspecting waterways shipping. Members of the Waterways Protection Police wore navy-blue uniforms with gold coloured buttons and insignia.

173.
Customs Service: Oberzollrat, 1938. Parade Uniform.

The German Customs Officers (Landzollbeamten) were divided into two distinct bodies, the Zollgrenzschutz or Customs and Border Protection and the Zollbeamten or Customs Officials. With the exception of the Waterways Customs Officials, who wore navy blue uniforms and gold insignia, the Customs and Border Protection and the Customs Officials wore the same basic uniforms with the same basic insignia. They were however distinguished from each other by the former having all their metal insignia, including the embroidery work of their badges, collar patches and shoulder straps in a dull grey colouring (gold for high ranking officials) whilst the latter body of men wore their insignia in bright aluminium or bright silver (gold also used for the insignia of their higher ranking officials). Both formations used dark bottle green as their facing and piping colour.

Both these organisations were under the jurisdiction of the Reich Finance Ministry but on 1 October 1944 the Customs and Border Protection service was transferred to be administered by Department IV of the Reich Security Main Office, the Gestapo. Their function together with the already existing Border Police (Grenzpolizei) was to guarantee the financial sovereignty of the Reich through border security measures. The Grenzpolizei was responsible for passport control at the borders, airports, roads and highways. It was entrusted with the entire normal border control.

174.
German Order Police: Lieutenant, Police Combat Regiment, 1943, Field Service Uniform.

For service outside the Reich frontiers, Barrack Police were formed into Police Regiments and Independent Battalions for the most part motorised and consisting of 500 to 550 men each, and organised and equipped on a military basis (see also Fig. 180). They served as security troops in all occupied countries and in an emergency, took part in military operations. They gained a reputation for extreme brutality and fanatical loyalty to Himmler and the Nazi regime.

Members of these Police Regiments and Independent Police Battalions wore the standard pattern Schutzpolizei uniforms supplemented with items of Army equipment. Camouflage clothing worn within these Police units was of the Waffen-SS style and camouflage patterning.

175.
German Police Formations: Bahnschutzpolizei-Gruppenführer, 1941, Service Uniform.

At the beginning of 1941 it was decided by the SS authorities, who were responsible for control of the Bahnschutzpolizei, to introduce two new types of uniforms for members of the Railway Protection Police to wear. One, manufactured in material of a soft blue-grey colour and intended for peace-time use and the other was to have been a field-grey version for use during the war. However, due to reasons of economy and for fear of possible confusion with the uniforms of the Army and Waffen-SS the field-grey version was suppressed. The blue-grey version however was produced, issued and worn by all ranks from the lowest 'Anwärter' up to the most senior official 'Chef der Bahnschutzpolizei'. Both a closed neck version of the tunic was produced as well as a jacket worn open at the neck, this necessitated in two sets of collar patches being produced, both patterns of which indicated the seven grades of Bahnschutzpolizei ranks. Nine different types of shoulder straps were used and no less than six variations of cuff-titles were worn, each one differing in design according to the rank grading of the wearer. All this was completed by two styles of hats, four types of chin straps or cords, three different arm eagles and sixteen various trade badges. It was obviously felt necessary to supply this variety of uniforms and insignias to be worn by men whose task it was simply to protect railway property and to maintain law and order on the German State Railway systems.

176.
German Police Formations: SS-Gruppenführer und Generalleutnant der Polizei Hans Weinreich, Chef der TeNo, 1942, Service Uniform.

Towards the end of 1942 senior members of Police formations were ordered by Himmler to wear SS style collar patches. Green was retained as the base colour and all embroidery work was carried out in gilt thread. Those ranks from SS-Brigadeführer u. Generalmajor der Polizei up to and including SS-Oberstgruppenführer u. Generaloberst der Polizei were affected. Whereas they had previously worn the style of collar patches as shown in Fig. 170 they now had to wear the appropriate SS pattern patches as shown here in Fig. 176.

177.
Reich Protection Police: Barrack Police Armoured Vehicle Crew Member, 1937. Overalls.

Kasernierte Polizei or Barrack Police was the term employed

to describe formations of the Schutzpolizei, generally in company strength, which were quartered in barracks in the larger towns and cities throughout Germany. They were equipped with armoured cars and weapons which in the main consisted of heavy and light machine-guns, sub-machine-guns, rifles, pistols and grenades.

Their function was to act as a mobile reserve for the ordinary Municipal Police when additional manpower was needed at any scenes of mass demonstrations, severe air raids or similar emergencies. They constituted a valuable arm of shock troops to supplement the National Socialist Party's own para-military formations. They could be described as the lineal descendants of the earlier Landespolizei, a para-military body of police permitted to Germany by the Treaty of Versailles (Fig. 181).

178.
Municipal Police: Motorised Gendarmerie Wachtmeister, 1937, Parade Uniform.

The Motorised Gendarmerie (Motorisierte Gendarmerie) was part of the Gendarmerie proper and was formed in 1936 to cope with the increase of traffic on the main and ordinary roads as well as the national autobahnen (see also Figure 166). Their jurisdiction was not limited by geographical divisions. They were organised throughout the Reich into Bereitschaft-en (Stand-by Squads) containing three or four platoons of men and vehicles each and which formed a mobile reserve available in barracks located at strategic points on the German highway system.

Troops of the Motorised Gendarmerie were distinguished by a chocolate brown cuff-title worn on the left sleeve of their tunic and bearing the silver embroidered words 'Motorisierte Gendarmerie'.

179.
German Order Police: Senior Inspector of Administration Police, 1938, Service Uniform.

The Administrative Police (Verwaltungspolizei) was the administrative branch of the ORPO, units of which were attached to Police agencies. Their various clerical record keeping and general administrative police functions included the enforcement of administrative regulations such as the supervision of buildings, theatres, factories, shops etc., the keeping of records, the writing of reports, taking of statements, registering of aliens, guarding of prisoners, and the issuing of permits, passports, licences etc., together with their inspection and regulation duties. Included in this administrative force were the Health Police (Gesundheitspolizei), the Factory and Shops Police (Gewerbepolizei) and the Building Police (Baupolizei). In smaller units members of the Schupo or Gendarmerie were called upon to carry out these functions. In large police stations and Reviere, however, personnel of the Verwaltungspolizei were stationed and entrusted with this work. They were regular civil service employees but were given extensive periods of training at Police Administrative Schools.

The small cloth badge worn above the left cuff on the tunic of the Polizei Oberinspektor (Fig. 179) known as the 'Kreuz des Südens' (Southern Cross) (see also Fig. 225) commemorated the traditions of former German colonial police troops inherited by Protection Police units in Kiel, Hamburg, Bremen, Berlin and Stuttgart.

180.
Reich Protection Police: Wachtmeister Police Tank Formations, 1944, Black Panzer Uniform.

Police Tank formations were a war-time extention of the Barrack Police (Kasernierte Polizei), see Fig. 177. Police crews of armoured vehicles were issued with the special black Panzer uniform, the same style of uniform as worn by the German Army's armoured formations, those of the Hermann Göring Division and the Waffen-SS.

The uniform carried Police insignia as shown in Fig. 180 and it was worn together with the black field replacement cap, also with police insignia.

181.
German Police Formations: Oberwachtmeister Landespolizeigruppe 'General Göring', 1935, Service Uniform.

The Protection Police formations in Prussia before June 1934 wore uniforms of dark blue (see Fig. 19). From that date all police uniforms were changed to what is referred to as 'police-green'. Members of the Landespolizeigruppe 'General Göring' had begun to wear their police-green uniforms a year earlier in July 1933. On 22 December 1933 the whole unit was authorised to wear on the left sleeve of their tunics and greatcoats a dark green cuff-title bearing the white cotton or silver-aluminium gothic lettering 'L.P.G. General Göring'. On 23 September 1935 the Land Police Group General Göring was officially transferred into the Luftwaffe to become the Regiment 'General Göring'. For a short period of six months from September 1935 to approximately February 1936, as a provisional measure until new Air Force uniforms became available, members of the LPG General Göring continued to wear their police-green uniforms but with the addition of Luftwaffe cap insignia and the Luftwaffe National Emblem worn on the right breast of their tunics (Fig. 181).

182.
German Police Formations: Penal Institution Strafenstaltsbeamte, 1940, Service Uniform.

The German prison system consisted of a) Ordinary Prisons

and b) Extraordinary Prisons. The ordinary prison system and penal institutions in Germany were administered by the Minister of Justice (Department V), which dealt with the administrative officials (Fig. 182) in charge of local institutions. The General-Staatsanwälte (Prosecutors) attached to the Oberlandesgerichte (High Courts) had certain supervisory functions. The ordinary prison system was administered largely by civil servants trained in penology, subject to the superimposed Nazi control. The German prison system comprised a number of types of prisons, including the following: Arbeitshaus for the detention and education of vagrants, prostitutes, etc., after service of sentence; Haftanstalt, for punishment of minor offences (Übertretungen); Jungendarrestanstalt, for punishment of minor youthful offenders; Jungendgefängnis, for punishment of youthful criminals; Sicherungsanstalt, for detention of habitual or dangerous criminals after service of sentence; Strafanstalt-Strafgefängnis, for adults sentenced to imprisonment; Zuchthaus, penitentiary for adults sentenced to penal servitude; Untersuchungsgefängnis-Untersuchungshaftanstalt, remand prison attached to a court, for detention of accused persons pending trial, also used for prisoners serving short sentences for minor offences.

The extraordinary prisons were a parallel system of prisons and concentration camps (Straflager) created during the Nazi regime for the express purpose of detaining party, political and racial prisoners. These were administered by Heinrich Himmler as head of the Security Police, (see Fig. 41 and Figs 127, 128, 170) through the Gestapo, with internal camp organisation of prisoners headed by habitual criminals of the worst type. They were conducted with systematic terrorism and brutality. The majority of internees were German political offenders and Jews, but there were also a number of ordinary criminals, military delinquents and non-Germans. A few special camps existed for women.

Officials of the German (ordinary) prison service, warders and adminsitrative personnel wore uniforms of police-green

191

with gold yellow insignia and carmine-red as their piping colour.

183.
German Police Formations: Female Police Auxiliary Helper, 1944, Service Dress.

Women had been employed in certain branches of the German police forces for many years. Their presence was necessary in the event of a female being arrested. They acted as female jailers in charge of women criminals. They were also employed more widely as telephone switchboard operators, secretaries and filing clerks, jobs at which they were particularly adept and which as the war progressed they took on in ever increasing numbers thereby filling the shortages in police manpower. They wore a simple uniform of police-green material. Their insignia consisted of the German Police eagle emblem worn on the front of their side caps and on the left upper arm or left cuff of their tunics (Fig. 183).

184, 185, 186.
Volkssturm: 184) NSDAP Political Leader (Gemeinschaftsleiter in Ortsgruppe). 185) Volkssturm Brigade Medical Officer. 186) Volunteer Youth, 1944, Germany.

Of all the measures taken to mobilize with speed the last manpower resources of the German nation, the most extreme was the creation of the Volkssturm, a national militia, designed to supplement the defence of the homeland.

A proclamation by Hitler announcing the formation of a German Volkssturm was broadcast by the German Radio on 18 October 1944, the date of the anniversary of the Battle of Leipzig in 1813. It stated that in all Gaue of the Greater German Reich a German Volkssturm comprising all able-bodied men from the ages of 16 to 60 not already in the

Armed Forces and able to bear arms was to be set up. This Volkssturm would defend German soil with all weapons and all means in so far as they were suitable to that purpose.

Gauleiters were entrusted with the establishment and command of the Volkssturm and in this task they were to be assisted by the most capable organisers and leaders of the National Socialist Party, the SA, the SS, the NSKK and the HJ.

SA Chief of Staff Wilhelm Scheppmann was appointed as Inspector of Rifle Training and NKSS-Korpsführer Erwin Kraus was to be Inspector of Motor Technical Training. Reichsführer-SS Heinrich Himmler in his capacity as Commander-in-Chief of the Replacement Army was made responsible for the military organisation, instructors, equipment and armament of the Volkssturm and Reichsleiter Martin Bormann was responsible for recruitment and political leadership.

All members of the Volkssturm were classed as 'Soldiers under the Army Code' for the duration of their service which was to take place locally wherever a given area was threatened.

Orders issued in this proclamation did not effect the affiliation of the Volkssturm members to other organisations. Service in the Volkssturm had priority over duty in all other Party organisations.

The Volkssturm was to be sent into the field according to Hitler's instructions issued by the Reichsführer-SS. All military by-laws concerning this decree were issued by Reichsführer-SS Himmler and all political by-laws by Reichsleiter Bormann.

As far as the Party was concerned the creation of the Volkssturm served a dual purpose. Firstly it strengthened the defences of the Reich, although in fact in many instances it proved to be more of an incumbrance, and secondly with the plot against Hitler's life still very fresh in the Party's mind it kept a large part of the population so thoroughly under military control that any incipient revolt against the Party at this late stage would have had a hard time thriving.

Although each Gauleiter was charged with the leadership, enrolment and organisation of the Volkssturm within his district, the largest Volkssturm units tended to correspond to the next smallest territorial sub-division of the Party organisation – the Kreis.

Through the card index system carefully kept by each Political Block Leader, the Party was well aware of the possible service potential of every male in Germany. However, the value of this levy 'en masse' was little more than an expression of the national will. The fighting ability of these Volkssturm units was practically nil. Lack of adequate weapons, ammunition and time for proper training, with units receiving only a few days and with some only a few hours instruction had its effect on morale. The desertion rate was high, both to the Allies and with many of the members drifting home when the opportunity presented itself. Fanatics did exist within the ranks and these tended to be members of the Hitler Youth.

Enthusiasm for the Volkssturm was almost non-existent even amongst the Volkssturmmänner themselves and especially from the regular troops and the civilian population. Opinion was that if the German Army could not stop the Allied advance into Germany what hope did the civilian Volkssturm have?

Volkssturm personnel were expected to furnish their own uniforms with even civilian, sports and working clothes being permitted. The only standard mark of identification being the wearing of an arm band, asserted by the Party to officially make the Volkssturm members a part of the Wehrmacht.

The official issue arm band is shown being worn in Fig. 185. Other variations existed and these too are illustrated.

Since practically every German had some sort of uniform the problem of supplying uniforms was not a great one. The SA brown uniforms were to have been dyed a different colour in order to prevent any possible equation of the

194

Volkssturm to a purely SA organisation. This, however, does not seem to have been done.

Despite the legality of civilian clothes being worn together with an officially issued arm band efforts were made to supply uniforms to those who had none and where possible to try and arrive at a semblance of a standard uniform for a given unit.

Practically anything was used including old Italian Army overcoats, Police uniforms stripped of insignia and even Imperial German uniforms. Army tunics with the national emblem removed were pressed into use. Rank insignia where it existed consisted of a matching pair of black collar patches with white metal pips arranged in the following pattern: without pips for Volkssturmmann, one pip for Gruppenführer, two pips horizontally for both Waffenmeister (Ordnance master) and Zahlmeister (Paymaster), three pips diagonally for Kompanieführer, Ordonnanceoffizier and Adjutant and four pips in a square pattern for Bataillonsführer. Pips were sometimes mounted directly into the collar of the garment without the use of collar patches (Fig. 185).

There was no remuneration for service in the Volkssturm, except when a member was taking part in actual combat. This together with the lack of a complete official uniform caused a great deal of disgruntlement throughout the Militia. Many of the members felt that they were assuming the duties of soldiers but with none of the privileges.

187, 188, 189, 190, 191, 192.
German Diplomatic and Government Officials: 187) Reichsaussenminister Joachim von Ribbentrop, 1939, Summer Undress Uniform. 188) German Ambassador von Ribbentrop, 1938, State Ceremonial Evening Dress. 189) Foreign Minister Joachim von Ribbentrop, 1941, Winter Full Dress. 190) Reichspräsidialrat Kiewitz, 1939, Full Dress. 191) Staatsminister und Chef der Präsidialkanzlei des Führers Dr Otto Meissner, 1939, Full Dress. 192) Diplomatic Official, 1941, Winter Full Dress.

The German Foreign Office, located at 74 to 76 Wilhelm-strasse, Berlin, was the official residence of Joachim von Ribbentrop. He had been the German Ambassador accredited to the Court of St James from 1936 to 1938. From 1938 to 1945 he was Germany's Foreign Minister. In this latter capacity he was responsible for greatly expanding the sphere of his ministerial interests. He established new branches in the Foreign Office which dealt with such matters as public information, legal, cultural, economic and political affairs. This increase in internal ministerial and external diplomatic matters resulted in two classifications of personnel, Foreign Office Diplomats and Governmental Officials. The rôle of the Diplomatic Corps was the maintenance of international dialogue at governmental level, the discussion with diplomats of other nations on all matters concerning treaties of international importance, the representation of German interests and the interests and welfare of German nationals living abroad. Government Officials were responsible for the administrative system of the Reich. There were fifteen ministeries operating under the Nazi regime:
1) Ministry of the Interior, 2) Foreign Affairs, 3) Public Enlightenment and Propaganda, 4) Finance, 5) Justice, 6) Economics, 7) Food and Agriculture, 8) Labour, 9) Armaments and War Production, 10) Science and Education, 11) Ecclesiastical Affairs, 12) Transport, 13) Post and Telegraph,

14) High Command of the Armed Forces, and 15) Air. Each of these was headed by a Minister assisted by one or more Under-Secretaries. Ministries were sub-divided into Departments (Abteilungen) usually under a Ministerial Director (Ministerialdirektor). These departments were in turn broken up into sections (Unterabteilungen) which were in charge of Sub-Directors (Ministerialdirigenten). Ministerial Councillors (Ministerialräte) and other officials and civil servants comprised the staffs of the component parts of the ministries.

All persons employed within these ministries wore uniform. Most senior members, usually at Ministerial and Under-Secretarial level, were permitted to wear civilian clothing when on duty at those times that did not require formal uniformed attire. All lesser officials and civil servants were obliged to wear their uniform for work at all time. The lower echelons naturally wore the uniform of the organisation from whence they came and not a Government Official's uniform. The basic colours used for uniforms worn by Diplomats and Governmental Officials were dark blue-black and light-grey, (see also the section on Eastern Territories Officials, Figs 193, 194). The light-grey uniform (Figs 189 & 191) was authorised only to be worn by Ministers and Officials attached to the Führer's Headquarters, and Officials serving in Military High Commands. In the Reich Protectorate of Bohemia and Moravia the grey uniform was worn only by the State Secretary, the Under State Secretary to the Reich Protector and all 'Oberlandräte' – administrative officials in the area of the Protectorate. The same grey uniform was permitted to be worn by the Governor-General in Poland (Generalgouvernement), his Deputy and all his district chiefs.

Colours were employed on dark blue-black uniforms to distinguish Senior Ministerial members as belonging to certain Ministries. Used as a foundation to the shoulder straps, as piping to the long trousers and as facing colours to the greatcoat, light-grey was used by General, Internal,

Financial and Special Administrative personnel. Justice Department administrative personnel wore wine red, Postal and Telegraph officials orange-red and Transportation personnel light red. Senior officials of the highest levels of authority were further distinguished from other lesser officials by having silver cording piped around the edge of their tunic and greatcoat collars (see Fig. 212). Four distinct pay groups of Diplomats and Government Officials existed, each permitted to wear their appointed insignia of his pay group on his uniform. A horseshoe shaped wreath of silver coloured oak leaves or plain bands of silver surmounted by an eagle and swastika emblem were worn on the left cuff of the tunic or greatcoat (Figs 188, 190, 192). Contained within the wreath was an arrangement of silver 'stars' which, depending on the number used being none to four, indicated administrative position. Other systems for indicating much the same information existed at different times (Fig. 191) and at the beginning of the war von Ribbentrop took to wearing an elaborate arm badge in gold showing a German eagle and swastika resting astride a globe representing the world all surrounded by a golden wreath of oakleaves (Fig. 189).

193, 194.
Eastern Territories Officials: 193) Gebietsassistenten, 1942, Undress Uniform. 194) Regierungsrat, 1943, Service Uniform.

During the first two years of the war on the Eastern Front the German ground forces had overrun vast areas of land. These conquered territories when added to the already annexed areas were to be the 'Lebensraum' of the new Greater Germany; the areas in the east that would eventually become the new living space for the expanding German population. It was intended that with the victorious conclusion of the war in Europe, the returning German warriors were to be rewarded for their dedication and sacrifices by being granted whole areas of this new land with the right to

198

farm and develop the rich soils of the Ukraine, eastern Poland, southern Russia, the Crimea and many other such provinces for their benefit and for the glory of the new Germany.

Towards this end a whole system of Government Officials, responsible for the running and maintenance of these German-held Eastern Territories, was set up under the auspices of Alfred Rosenberg and his Reichsministerium für die besetzten Ostgebiete, the Reich Ministry for the Occupied Eastern Territories (RMBO). As was the case with all German uniformed organisations a complex system of ranks and appointments was set up which was reflected in the uniforms and differences in insignia worn by the many grades of these Eastern Territorial Officials or Ostbeamten. A series of uniform items was designed by the famous Berlin artist-designer Egon Jantke.

They were made up from large stocks of material originally intended for SA uniforms but during the war were no longer required. The use of this suitable dyed material produced jackets, tunics and greatcoats in a golden-brown colouring which gave rise to the officials being nick-named 'Golden Pheasants'. Insignia, buttons and braiding were in either silver or gold, depending on rank and four colours were used to indicate levels of official responsibility; Bordeaux red for Gebietskommissariat; Orange red for Hauptkommissariat; Carmine red for Reichskommissariat and Bright red for Ministerial Officials. The decision as to whether to issue a white summer uniform was held in abeyance until the end of the war. It took some time for the actual insignia worn on the uniforms and the accoutrements worn with the uniforms to be sorted out. At first the large silver arm eagle shown in Fig. 194 was originally worn for a very short period only above the right breast pocket of the tunics and jackets. The cap insignia was an almost straight copy of that worn by German Diplomatic and Government Officials (see Figs 190, 191, 192), doubtless because these Eastern Territorial Officials were considered an extension of the German Diplomatic Service and were akin to German Government Officials.

195.
Eastern Territories Officials: Construction Unit Officer, 1943, Service Dress.

The Baudienst im Generalgouvernement was just one of a number of uniformed bodies that operated in the Eastern Territories. The Construction Service in the General Government – the Nazi German name given to occupied Poland – was a unit officered by Germans and staffed by Poles that carried out construction and land reclamation work on much the same lines as that performed by the Reichsarbeitsdienst. The majority of the Polish workers were poorly clothed. They wore, during the summer months, trousers made from German flour sacks, shirts and cloth caps of civilian origin. The German overseers were better dressed in that they wore a properly tailored uniform with regulation pattern peaked cap both of which displayed insignia.

196, 197 & 198.
Reich Air Protection League: 196) RLB Leutnant, 1937, Greatcoat. 197) Honorary Präsident of the RLB, General of Infantry von Roques, 1938, Parade Uniform. 198) RLB Blockwart, 1939, Service Uniform.

The Reich Air Protection League – Reichsluftschutzbund or RLB – was founded on 28 April 1933 by Hermann Göring, Generalleutnant Grimm and Major Waldschmitt who headed the Präsidium. It was organised into fifteen Landesgruppen with each of these divided into Ortsgruppen. Local police stations were everywhere used as recruiting offices. Civil Defence propaganda and training measures throughout the Reich were handled by the RLB under the supervision of the Air Ministry. The work of the Air Defence League was supported by manufacturers of gas masks, chemicals and building materials who advertised their products in the League's two original periodicals *Der Reichsluftschutz* and *Deutsche Flugillustrierte*. These two publications were superseded by a single, illustrated fortnightly publication called *Die Sirene*. This contained articles, adverts and official instructions. The League supervised all civil defence training throughout Germany which included practical demonstrations, lectures and film shows. The membership of the RLB numbered over twenty million.

The facing colour used by the RLB was lilac, a colour not used by any other Third Reich uniformed organisation. It appeared as the colour used on the League's collar patches (Fig. 196), as shoulder strap underlay and as piping to tunics and trousers. The RLB had a variety of arm bands, usually in blue and very often displaying the star-burst emblem of the RLB (Fig. 198).

199, 200, 201.
Security and Help Services and Air Raid Warning Service: 199) SHD–Mann, 1943, Duty Uniform. 200) SHD–Zugführer, 1944, Service Uniform. 201) LSW–Zugführer, 1945, Service Uniform.

As part of the German defence system built up to minimise the effects of enemy air raids two organisations existed, amongst many others, that could be said to have been created as a direct result of aerial bombing. The Sicherheits und Hilfsdienst – the Security and Help Service, SHD, and the Luftschutz Warndienst or Air Raid Warning Service, LSW.

The SHD was a conscripted force of men housed in barracks on a rotating basis. That is to say they were allowed to sleep at home every other night, air raids permitting. Service in the SHD was a form of 'reserved occupation' in that it meant its members were exempted from having to serve in the Armed Forces. They were also exempt from doing physical training or rifle drill. They were not however permitted to pursue any other occupation whilst serving in the SHD.

201

The Security and Help Services were highly mobile and they had transportation for both people and animals. Their equipment included pile drivers, hydraulic jacks, cutting equipment and wrecking tools. There were five branches of the SHD: 1) Decontamination Squads, 2) Fire Fighting service, (Fig. 199), 3) Repair Work Units, 4) Veterinary service, and 5) Medical units. Qualified persons in any of these five units wore an oval cloth badge with the initial letter on a coloured background on the left sleeve of their tunics (Fig. 199).

The LSW was an important organisation that acted in much the same way as Great Britain's Royal Observer Corps in that their observers kept watch during daylight hours for approaching enemy aircraft. At all times, day and night, they analysed incoming reports from other LSW units, from the Police and Flugmeldedienst units (see Fig. 150) on the progress of bomber formations over Germany and it was on their conclusions that the air raid warnings were sounded alerting the local population of an impending air attack. They also worked in close unison with the Police authorities during the coordinating of air raid and post-air raid services. The LSW was also responsible for giving the 'all clear' signal.

Both organisations wore Air Force style uniforms in blue-grey with off white fatigue clothing being issued for heavy duty work. Their insignia was very similar in that it was dark green in colour. The letters SHD appeared on the collar patches of the Security and Help Services (Fig. 200) and on the patches worn by personnel of the Air Raid Warning Service were the letters LSW (Fig. 201).

202, 203, 204.
Factory Police: 202) Factory Police Officer, 1942, Service Uniform. 203) Factory Police Guard, 1942, Service Uniform. 204) Factory Police NCO, 1944, Service Uniform.

Factory Protection Police, known as 'Werksschutzpolizei'

were persons privately employed by industrial concerns to act as factory guards and watchmen. Unlike many of the other police organisations operating in Germany at this time the Werksschutzpolizei were subject only to regulations issued by the Air Ministry and not by the police authorities. The pattern of the uniforms provided for these factory guards was of the usual style for jackets, tunics (open and closed neck), trousers, breeches, greatcoats and headdress. The colour of these uniforms was usually either darkish grey or blue-black. The Werksschutz emblem was worn on the peaked cap by members of most concerns (Figs 203, 202, 204) and in almost all cases the Werksschutz arm badge was also worn (Figs 202, 203). Factory Police could, in some instances, be identified as belonging to a particular company by the use of collar patches which displayed the company's logo or emblem (Figs 202, 203).

205, 206, 207, 208, 209, 210.
German Red Cross: 205) Senior Nursing Sister, 1937, Service Dress. 206) Red Cross Watch Leader, 1937, Formal Dress. 207) Red Cross Man, 1937, Duty Uniform. 208) Red Cross Nurse, 1942, Hospital Uniform. 209) German Red Cross General, 1944, Greatcoat. 210) Nursing Sister, 1942, Tropical uniform.

Germany had possessed a Red Cross organisation for almost seventy years from the time when it was first established in 1864. Like the majority of those organisations that existed in Germany prior to the Nazis coming to power the German Red Cross (Deutsche Rote Kreuz) was brought into line with other uniformed bodies. Its organisational structure was altered, its uniforms were re-designed and its insignia of rank, qualification badges and decorations reflected both the National Socialist control as well as the new and complex rank structure.

The colour traditionally used for Red Cross uniforms, other than the white nursing clothing, had always been slate-grey. This was retained when in 1937 a range of new clothing for nursing sisters, medical officers and medical attendants was introduced.

Male personnel showed their ranks by means of a system of shoulder straps. Bars of silver lace in varying numbers and thicknesses were worn on the tunic sleeve to indicate the length of service held by the wearer. Nurses and Sisters displayed their rank insignia by a system of pips worn on the corners of the collar of either their white blouse or slate-grey tunics depending on grade. These pips were in blue for the white blouse worn by the lower ranks, and silver or gold for the more senior females. A series of coloured enamelled brooches were worn by the nursing sister to indicate various grades of nursing qualification.

Few changes were made during the course of the war years to the uniforms first introduced in 1937. The most notable exception being the introduction later of a tropical uniform for use by Nursing Sisters who were to work with the German forces in North Africa and other hot climate countries. Their uniform (see Fig. 210) consisted of a light brown tropical jacket and matching skirt. To this was added a sun helmet.

The greatcoat as worn by General Officers of the German Red Cross was distinguished by having pale dove-grey lapel facings, the same colour material as was used for the Red Cross collar patches which bore a small red enamelled cross and which were worn by all male Red Cross personnel regardless of rank.

211, 212, 213, 215.
Organisation Todt: 211) Haupttruppführer, 1941, Undress Uniform. 212) Reichsminister für Bewaffnung und Munition, Professor Albert Speer, 1943, OT Ministerial Uniform. 213) OT-Frontarbeiter, 1940, Duty Uniform. 215) OT-Einsatzgruppenleiter I, 1944, Service Uniform.

The Organisation Todt or OT was yet another prime example of a uniformed organisation, created during the time of the Third Reich, which had no historical connection and it was during its period of existence constantly altering its uniform styles, rearranging its rank terms and changing its rank insignia. The Organisation Todt was created and originally directed by Dr Fritz Todt. As a qualified civil engineer it was he who was responsible before the war for the construction of much of the Autobahn system throughout Germany and for the building of the German 'West Wall' defensive system known as the Siegfried Line. In 1940 he was appointed as Minister of Armaments, a position he held until his death in an aircraft crash in 1942. As Armaments Minister he was succeeded by Albert Speer (Fig. 212). Speer was born in 1905. He was an architect by profession. He joined the Nazi Party in 1932 and on succeeding Professor Troost he became Hitler's personal architect in 1934. He designed the New Reich Chancellery built in Berlin together with the Nürnberg Kongresshalle and other major works. In 1942 on the death of Fritz Todt he was appointed Minister of War Production and Armaments and was also made responsible for State construction work. He proved to be an extremely able organiser, so much so that production and output of war material increased during the years 1943–44 far beyond what had previously been achieved despite the massive Allied bombing offensive levelled against German industry. As a Minister of State Speer wore a uniform similar to that worn by senior OT officials but without OT rank insignia. Silver cording worn around the edge of the collar indicated his

Ministerial position (Fig. 212. See also Figs 187–189.)

OT construction workers, once war had broken out, found themselves in front-line situations. It was necessary to arm the German personnel in order that they could defend themselves against surprise attacks from the enemy or partisans. Efforts were made so that every German worker, regardless of age, received some instruction in the use of weapons, mostly small arms. Equipment was scarce, most of it going to the regular Armed Forces so that OT units were forced to make do with whatever captured or obsolete stocks they could lay their hands on (Fig. 213). OT Einsatzgruppen (Work Groups) were employed in construction work in France (the Atlantic Wall etc), Italy (various defensive positions) and the Low Countries. The OT co-operated closely with German and foreign private construction and supply firms and as the war progressed made full use of ever increasing numbers of foreign workers, sometimes slave labour. The transport system used by the Organisation Todt was maintained by the NSKK.

214.
Technische Nothilfe: Unterwachtmeister der TN, 1945, Fatigue Uniform.

For heavy duty work such as clearing rubble or working in difficult and dirty areas a fatigue uniform of strong, drill material consisting of a jacket and shapeless trousers was issued to TeNo personnel. They wore their TeNo arm eagle emblem on the left upper arm and the black and grey 'Technische Nothilfe' cuff-title on the left sleeve (see also Figs 217, 218 219 & 276).

216.
Transportkorps Speer: Stabskapitän, 1944, Service Uniform.

At the begining of hostilities NSKK transport units were

attached to Army and Luftwaffe formations in an effort to supplement the transportation of these regular front-line troops. As the war developed even more NSKK units participated and they became organised, first into Regiments (NSKK-Transport-Regiment 'Luftwaffe' for example), later into Groups and Brigades (NSKK-Transportgruppe 'Todt' and NSKK-Transportbrigade 'Speer') and finally in 1944 they were all grouped together under one title 'Transport-korps Speer', with its Regiments going to the Luftwaffe and the Army.

Late in 1944 a new olive-brown coloured uniform was introduced for all ranks of the 'Transportkorps Speer' (Fig. 216). It had aluminium buttons, brown collar and collar patches of an unusual design displaying the stylised letters 'SP' on both patches. Rank was indicated by the shoulder straps. SP Army units wore the Army pattern national emblem over the right breast pocket.

217, 218, 219.
Technical Emergency Corps: 217) TeNo Scharführer, 1940, Greatcoat. 218) TeNo Hauptbereitschaftsführer, General Service Branch, 1944, Undress Uniform. 219) TeNo Vormann, 1942, Field Service (Armed Forces) Uniform.

The Technical Emergency Corps or Technische Nothilfe (TeNo) founded in September 1919 by the Weimar Government functioned as a strike-breaking organisation which concerned itself chiefly with maintaining vital public services. During the latter years of the Republic when there were few strikes it was used mainly as a technical reserve in case of natural catastrophe. After 1933 it was reorganised as a national force and in 1937 it was incorporated into the Ordnungspolizei. Its main task was to cope with all emergencies and dangers to the public with emphasis on gas and air defence. During the war its rôle was extended to provide technically trained personnel for emergency work and to deal with breakdowns in public services. The bulk of their work was of an air raid defence nature with the emphasis on protecting vital public utility services. In addition to this home front work units of the TeNo known as TeNo Kommandos operated with the Wehrmacht employed on construction and repair work. They were often used on a large scale in military operations for repairing damage, clearing waterways, repairing lock-gates, operating pumping stations and generating plants amongst other skilled and important tasks. Portions of these TeNo Kommandos were incorporated into the German Army and Air Force as technical troops (Technische Truppen) which eventually lost their identity as TeNo units entirely.

The pre-war uniforms worn by TeNo personnel were dark navy-blue (Figs 217 & 218). Its use during the war years declined and it tended to be restricted to those persons already possessing it. For the purposes of both pre-war and war-time work involving TeNo troops when the work was of a hard or dirty nature an off white herringbone drill suit of jacket and trousers was issued as a work uniform (see Fig. 214). The field-grey Armed Forces style uniform was worn by TeNo units operating in the field assisting with tasks for the German Forces (Fig. 219). Worn with the Field Service TeNo uniform by those personnel attached to the Armed Forces was the yellow armband bearing the black gothic lettering 'Deutsche Wehrmacht'. This was a common practice used by a number of German para-military formations or foreign, non-German volunteer units when serving in the field as the use of this arm band, it was claimed, established the wearer as a genuine member of the German Armed Forces entitled to the same privileges as afforded to regular German armed forces personnel (Fig. 219, see also Fig. 73 and similarly Figs 184, 185 & 186).

The TeNo had four branches all of which were distinguished by the use of four different colours. Blue was used by the Technical Service Branch, Technischedienst or TD, red for the Air Raid Protection Service Branch, the Luftschutzdienst or LD, orange-yellow for the Emergency Service, the Bereitschaftsdienst or BD and green for the General Service or Allgemeiner Dienst, AD. The colours were used on the coloured side arm knots by TeNo men and NCOs and as piping to the collar of the dark blue tunics by officers (Fig. 218).

Those TeNo personnel who had successfully passed through the TeNo Reich Training School were permitted to wear on their left upper sleeve of their tunics and greatcoats the silver and black TeNo Tyr-rune emblem.

220, 222.
German Forestry Service: 220) Oberjägermeister, 1936, Ceremonial Uniform. 222) Reichsjägermeister, 1934, Forestry Uniform.

Forest and Game administration, formerly under the control of the Länder or individual German states, were united by the Nazis into the Office of the Forest Master (Reichsforstamt) under the control of Hermann Göring as Chief Forester and Hunting Master of the German Reich. Before the war there were 869,300 persons employed in the forestry and wood-working industry. Those responsible for the conservation of game and the management of the forests were organised into a uniformed body, sub-divided into an ascending system of responsibility marked by the use of collar insignia and shoulder straps.

Green was chosen for the colour of the Forestry and Falconry Service uniforms with green leather belts, dark green collar facings and piping and, with those forms of dress used for work in the forest, green shirts with green ties were worn. On the left upper arm of their tunics, blouses and greatcoats, Forestry Officials wore a dark green oval badge which displayed the skull of a deer with a full set of antlers worked in silver wire (gold for most senior ranks) and in which was set a black swastika surrounded by and emitting fine silver (or gold) rays. Behind the skull was positioned a

209

scroll bearing the initial letters D.J. standing for Deutsche Jägerschaft.

221.
German Falconry Order: Gaumeister, 1938, Service Dress.

The Falconry Order was brought into being in 1938. Members of the Order wore a style of uniform identical to that worn by the Forestry Service personnel. They were however distinguished by wearing special collar insignia and an arm badge. This arm badge displayed a hooded falcon standing within a wreath of oakleaves set against a rising sun symbol and standing on a scroll bearing the initial letters D.F.O., Deutsche Falkenorden.

223, 224.
National Socialist War Victims and Former Soldiers Associations: 223) Official, National Socialist War Victims Support Service, 1939, Service Suit; 224) Official, National Socialist Empire War Association, 1938, Service Suit.

The origins of the German Soldiers Welfare Organisations that existed during the Third Reich were said to have originated in the year 1786 when Fusiliers from the Army of Frederick the Great created the first Comrades Fellowship in an effort to help one another. After the First World War, with so many of Germany's men having served in the armed forces, there was a great and obvious revival of interest in this type of organisation. The Steel Helmet (Stahlhelm – see Figs 38, 39) organisation existed which amongst other things was a mutual help organisation of former soldiers as was the Lighthouse Association of the German Land Warfare Association (Kyffhäuserbund der deutschen Landkriegerverbande, KfHB) and the Reichstreubund (Empire Loyalists) amongst others. The Nazi Party created their own organisation known as the National Socialist Empire War Association (Nationalsozialistches Reichskriegerbund NS-RKB) which on 4 March 1938 became the only permitted organisation whilst at the same time absorbing into its ranks the membership of the other abolished associations (Fig. 224). For this purpose the Reich was organised into eighteen Provincial Groups (Gaukriegerverbände) divided into 850 Districts (Kreiskriegerverbände) which were in turn subdivided into 41,000 local Groups (Kriegerkameradschaften) comprising in all more than 3,000,000 former soldiers. This organisation was headed by the Reichskriegerführer, General of Infantry and SS-Gruppenführer Reinhard with its Honorary Leader (Ehrenführer) Reichsstatthalter General of Infantry Ritter von Epp.

The National Socialist War Victims Support Service (Nationalsozialistisches Kriegsopferversorgung – NSKOV) was a purely Nazi Party organisation set up to help and assist in the welfare of victims of the First World War as well as those members of the Party that had suffered during the early periods of fighting with the Communists (Fig. 223).

Both these organisations wore civilian style suits to which were pinned metal badges and medals and on which the membership wore arm bands and cuff-titles. Like all uniformed organisations these 'Old Soldier' associations had a complex system of ranks and rank insignia and they wore badges awarded for various skills at shooting and marksmanship.

225.
German East Africa former Colonial Servicemen's Association: Official of the Deutsche Kolonialkriegerbund, 1934, Tradition Uniform.

German troops who had served in the former armed forces of the East African and other German colonies were formed into a separate Kameradschaft as part of the NS-

Reichskriegerbund. They had all the rights and performed all the duties of a regular NS-RK Bund local group but in place of the standard dress of a dark civilian suit and peaked cap they were permitted to wear their former colonial forces uniform with its very distinctive wide brimmed, felt hat (Fig. 225).

226, 227, 228, 229, 230, 231.
German State Railways: 226) Central Office Secretary, 1937, Open neck Service Jacket. 227) Communications Official, 1944, Greatcoat. 228) Senior Locomotive Driver, 1941, Walking-out Uniform. 229) Survey Inspector, 1942. Closed neck Service Tunic. 230) Female Auxiliary Worker, 1944, Female Service Uniform. 231) Railway Assistant, 1943, Service Tunic.

The Deutsche Reichsbahn, the German State Railways, was a nationally-owned undertaking which had a considerable measure of financial, administrative and operating autonomy. It was a public service operated on a self-supporting financial basis as laid down by the Reichsbahn Law of 1939. In 1938 the railway system covered about 35,000 route miles of standard gauge track of which 1,500 miles were electrically operated. Well equipped with locomotives and rolling stock, its construction standards were high and its operating efficiency very good. The Reichsbahn was a first class railway system comparable in every way with the major systems of Great Britain and the United States. Since 1937 the Reichsbahn expanded with the conquests of the Reich. The inclusion of the railway systems of Czechoslovakia, Austria, Poland, Alsace-Lorraine, Memel and Luxembourg brought the total route length directly controlled and operated from 35,000 miles to about 50,000 miles. The number of locomotives and amount of rolling stock increased proportionately. The total number of employees rose from 800,000 in 1937 to 1,400,000 in 1942 with the expansion of the Reichsbahn at its height.

The uniforms worn by members of the German State Railways during the period 1933 to 1945 were in many respects similar in general appearance to those worn during the Weimar period. The same basic colours of dark blue jackets, tunics and greatcoats worn together with black trousers were continued under the new regime, as was the use of black collar patches and red and yellow as the colours for piping and insignia. Railway uniforms of the Third Reich period were subjected to a number of new introductions and changes in existing styles but it was the insignia displayed on these uniforms that tended to be changed with far more frequency and for a variety of reasons.

Being a non-military uniformed organisation the command structure of the German State Railways did not have a 'rank system' based on military lines. Instead it was divided into four main 'Worker Classifications' and sub-divided into twenty-three pay groups containing eighty-three different grades of Officials from the lowest Administration Aspirant up to the Director of the State Railways. Generally speaking the visual identification of the gradings to these twenty-three pay groups was achieved by the use of individual shoulder straps which indicated the wearers' pay group level whilst the use of collar patches and cap cords were used to distinguish the main Worker Classification. Individual trade or specialist skills were marked by the use of specialist cloth badges also worn on the uniforms. More precisely, however, the whole system of shoulder straps, collar patches and to a lesser extent cap cords and cap insignia underwent two major changes which drastically altered the original system. Originally when first introduced in March 1936 only shoulder straps were used to indicate the wearers' pay group. The basic collar patch design was the same for all Reichsbahn personnel (Fig. 226). On 13 February 1941 this was changed when the universal collar patch system of a gilt coloured metal winged wheel mounted on to a red piped, black patch was changed. A whole new system of collar patches was introduced designed to indicate the four main levels of worker classifications. Two patterns of these new collar patches were produced for each of the four levels, one pattern for use on the closed neck tunics (Figs 227, 229, 231) and the other type for use on tunics and jackets worn open at the neck (Fig. 228). The existing shoulder straps continued in use as before but with slight modifications in design.

A few months later during the summer of 1941 it was the turn of the shoulder strap system to be changed when they were done away with completely and a new innovation of 'Passant' shoulder insignia introduced (Fig. 227). These 'Passant' shoulder bars were very similar in principle but different in construction and colouring to the modern United States Army officers' shoulder ornaments (shoulder straps) as worn on the US Army Blue Uniform. The second pattern collar patches remained to be used together with these 'Passants' (Fig. 227). However, true to most uniformed organisations, all these innovations became completely mixed and although dates were laid down by the Reichsbahn clothing authorities for the discontinuation and introduction of old and new insignia, and most probably because this action was meant to be staggered over a period of time by the various pay group levels, many items of obsolete uniforms and insignia continued in use long after their date of withdrawal and even up to the end of the war.

Another important but short-lived item of insignia was also introduced in February 1941, namely a cuff-title (Fig. 228). This item (and there were a number of differing titles) was intended to be worn together with the eagle and swastika arm badge (Fig. 228) but these items were replaced within months by the more familiarly named arm badges (Fig. 231).

232, 233, 234.
German Postal Service: 232) Postbetriebsassistent, 1939, Service Uniform. 233) Postal Protection Service, Postschutz Gruppenführer, 1940, Service Uniform. 234) Post Woman, 1940, Service clothing.

German postal, telegraph and telephone services together with some aspects of radio services were combined in an autonomous organisation which functioned under the designation 'Deutsche Reichspost'.

Male employees who were fully qualified functionaries were entitled and obliged to wear the full official Reichspost uniform when on duty. The uniform consisted of a dark blue jacket and black trousers. Rank was shown by the use of collar patches of which there were a series of twenty different collar patch designs. Orange was used as the piping colour (Fig. 232).

Women were employed within the German Postal Service in a number of capacities. Before 1940 those of them who were not qualified as full functionaries, that is qualified Postal officials entitled to wear the full regulation uniform, were only permitted to wear the 'Reichspost' arm band (see Fig. 236), the peaked cap and rain cape when on duty. After 1940 however, a uniform was introduced for their use (Fig. 234). This consisted of a blue jacket worn with the woman's own civilian blouse, matching coloured skirt or slacks and worn with a dark blue beret and black shoes. No Postal insignia other than the 'Deutsche Reichspost' arm badge was worn and only the small white metal cap eagle appeared by law on the orange piped beret.

The Postal Protection Service or Postschutz was organised in March 1933. It was given the responsibility of protecting and maintaining the security of all post offices and postal establishments together with all mail, telephone and telegraph services throughout Germany. Prior to 1942 the Postschutz was under the control of the Reich Ministry of Post and Telegraph. In March 1942, upon the approval of

Hitler, the Postschutz was incorporated into the Allgemeine-SS and was then designated as SS-Postschutz.

Members of the Postschutz wore uniforms of field-grey with orange as the colour used for their collar patches and special arm insignia (Fig. 233). After the organisation was taken over by the General-SS the same uniform continued to be worn but with SS style collar insignia.

235, 237.
German Tram, 'Bus and Auxiliary Postal Services: 235) Auxiliary Omnibus Conductress, Berlin Transport Company, 1944, Topcoat. 237) Tram Driver/Conductor Cologne Transport Company, 1941, Working Uniform.

The subject of uniformed clothing as worn by the employees of German Omnibus, Tramway and Underground passenger transport companies is by its nature complex and extensive. Most German towns with a population of ten thousand or over were serviced by trams and buses and in the capital by the U-Bahn or underground railway system. Most of these transport systems were almost entirely owned in whole or in part by Municipal Corporations, the most important of which was the Reich capital's 'Berliner Verkehrsgesellschaft'. A comparatively free hand was allowed these various communal transport companies with regard to the uniforms and work clothing they issued to their employees.

Since 1936 all employees of all transport companies were obliged to wear the German national emblem (Eagle and Swastika) on their uniform headdress. The uniforms themselves were not allowed to be produced in any of the 'protected uniform colours', that is in Army field-grey, Air Force blue-grey or the brown of the Party's political formations. Insignia of 'rank' was left to the individual company but during the war there was an attempt made to unify the various methods. The actual cut of the tunics, jackets (closed or open neck), trousers, blouses, skirts, slacks and greatcoats and topcoats was left up to the companies. In Vienna in 1941 female auxiliaries working as conductresses on the city's tramway system were even permitted to wear the company's regulation service blouse in a choice of colours in beige, grey and light blue, to match the colour of their hair.

The basic personnel structure of most transport companies was usually divided into two branches. Those persons who drove, conducted or maintained vehicles and those that administered the running of these vehicles. The rank system of each classification was indicated by insignia worn on their regulation uniforms.

236.
Auxiliary Postal Workers: BDM Auxiliary Post Girl, 1943, BDM Suedette Tunic and Melton cloth skirt.

Shortage of manpower forced many of the State organisations to make increasing use of women and to a certain extent of young girls to try and make good the deficiencies in their work force. Older members of the rank and file BDM were persuaded to volunteer for a whole range of jobs in an effort to keep these essential services moving. The delivery and sorting of mail was just one such job (see also Fig. 63). It was impossible to provide all these auxiliary workers with a regulation uniform. As an expediency the issue of arm bands bearing a design peculiar to the parent body was a common method of overcoming this problem. The BDM girl acting as a postal worker delivering mail is wearing such a 'Reichspost' arm band.

238, 239.
German Coal Miners: 238) Mining Overseer. 239) Mining Official, 1938.

The importance of the miner has for many years been

217

recognised throughout Germany and as a reflection of this importance, and on those occasions that were considered to be of a festive or important nature, the mining personnel would set aside their work clothes and put on their traditional miners dress uniform.

A version of this uniform which is featured in Figs 238 and 239 evolved, as is usually the way with traditional costume, from the styles of dress worn originally by miners in most of the mining provinces of Germany of at least two hundred years ago, and in appearance it has an affinity with military attire.

In some districts of Germany after the middle of the eighteenth century regulations were laid down as to its appearance. Leather aprons and leather knee pieces became a feature of the earlier dress uniforms. When marching or in procession miners carried axes with slender handles (238), swords were worn by musicians, and the distinctive peakless shako complete with brush or feathered plume became almost a trade mark.

During the period of the Third Reich the only visible acquiescence made to the new regime as far as the full dress uniform was concerned was the use of the swastika arm band.

Although each mining district had its variations in detail and to a lesser extent in colourings, in the main the German miner was distinguished by the use of jet black uniforms decorated with black velvet trimmings, no doubt chosen as an appropriate colouring considering the nature of their work.

240.
German Coal Miners: Apprentice Miner 1942.

The mining apprentice wore a uniform similar to that of his elders but it was not quite so elaborate. The peaked cap was a form of head–dress, a concession to modern dress, that was also available to all other mining personnel.

Chart of Comparative Ranks

#	British Army:	US Army:	German Army:	German Navy
1	Private	Private	Grenadier	Matrose
2		Private 1st class	Obergrenadier	Matrosengefreiter
3	Lance-Corporal		Gefreiter	Matrosenobergefreiter
			Obergefreiter	Matrosenhauptgefreiter
			Stabsgefreiter	Matrosenstabsgefreiter
4	Corporal	Corporal	Unteroffizier	Maat
5	Sergeant	Sergeant	Unterfeldwebel	Obermaat
6			Fähnrich	Fähnrich zur See
7		Staff Sergeant	Feldwebel	Feldwebel
8	Company Sergeant Major	Master Sergeant	Oberfeldwebel	Stabsfeldwebel
			Hauptfeldwebel	Oberfeldwebel
9			Oberfähnrich	Oberfähnrich zur See
10	Regimental Sergeant Major	Warrant Officer	Stabsfeldwebel	Stabsoberfeldwebel
11	Second Lieutenant	Second-Lieutenant	Leutnant	Leutnant zur See
12	First-Lieutenant	First-Lieutenant	Oberleutnant	Oberleutnant zur See
13	Captain	Captain	Hauptmann/Rittmeister	Kapitänleutnant
14	Major	Major	Major	Korvettenkapitän
15	Lieutenant Colonel	Lieutenant-Colonel	Oberstleutnant	Fregattenkapitän
16	Colonel	Colonel	Oberst	Kapitän zur See
				Kommodore
17	Brigadier	Brigadier-General	Generalmajor	Vizeadmiral
18	Major General	Major-General	Generalleutnant	Konteradmiral
19	Lieutenant General	Lieutenant-General	General der Infanterie usw.	Admiral
20	General	General	Generaloberst	Generaladmiral
21	Field Marshal	General of the Army	Generalfeldmarschall	Grossadmiral
22				

	German Air Force	Waffen-SS	Police – Schupo	SA
1	Flieger/Soldat	SS-Schütze		SA-Sturmmann
2		SS-Oberschütze		
3	Gefreiter	SS-Sturmmann		SA-Obersturmmann
	Obergefreiter	SS-Rottenführer		SA-Rottenführer
	Hauptgefreiter			
	Stabsgefreiter			
4	Unteroffizier	SS-Unterscharführer	Unterwachtmeister	SA-Scharführer
5	Unterfeldwebel	SS-Scharführer	Wachtmeister	SA-Oberscharführer
6				
7	Feldwebel	SS-Oberscharführer	Oberwachtmeister	SA-Truppführer
			Revierwachtmeister	
8	Oberfeldwebel	SS-Hauptscharführer	Hauptwachtmeister	SA-Obertruppführer
		SS-Stabsscharführer		SA-Haupttruppführer
9				
10	Stabsfeldwebel	SS-Sturmscharführer		
11	Leutnant	SS-Untersturmführer	Polizei Meister	SA-Sturmführer
			Polizei Obermeister	
			Polizei Leutnant	
12	Oberleutnant	SS-Obersturmführer	Schupo Inspektor	SA-Obersturmführer
			Oberleutnant	
13	Hauptmann	SS-Hauptsturmführer	Hauptmann	SA-Hauptsturmführer
14	Major	SS-Sturmbannführer	Major	SA-Sturmbannführer
15	Oberstleutnant	SS-Obersturmbannführer	Oberstleutnant	SA-Obersturmbannführer
16	Oberst	SS-Standartenführer	Oberst	SA-Standartenführer
		SS-Oberführer		SA-Oberführer
17	Generalmajor	SS-Brigadeführer	Generalmajor	SA-Brigadeführer
18	Generalleutnant	SS-Gruppenführer	Generalleutnant	SA-Gruppenführer
19	General der Flieger usw.	SS-Obergruppenführer	General der Polizei	SA-Obergruppenführer
20	Generaloberst	SS-Obergruppenführer	Generaloberst der Pol.	
21	Generalfeldmarschall	Reichsführer-SS		
22	Reichsmarschall			Stabschef der SA

	Hitlerjugend	RAD	RADwJ	NSKK
1	Hitlerjunge	Arbeitsmann	Arbeitsmaid	NSKK-Sturmmann
2		Arbeitsmann		NSKK-Obersturmmann
3	Rottenführer	Vormann		NSKK-Rottenführer
		Obervormann		
		Hauptvormann		
4	Kameradschaftsführer	Truppführer	Kameradschaftsälteste	NSKK-Scharführer
5	Oberkameradschaftsführer			NSKK-Oberscharführer
6				
7	Scharführer	Obertruppführer	Jungführerin	NSKK-Truppführer
8	Oberscharführer			NSKK-Obertruppführer
				NSKK-Haupttruppführer
9		Unterfeldmeister	Maidenunterführerin	
10				
11	Gefolgschaftsführer	Feldmeister	Maidenführerin	NSKK-Sturmführer
12	Obergefolgschaftsführer	Oberfeldmeister	Maidenoberführerin	NSKK-Obersturmführer
13	Hauptgefolgschaftsführer	Oberstfeldmeister	Maidenhauptführerin	NSKK-Hauptsturmführer
14	Stammführer	Arbeitsführer	Stabsführerin	NSKK-Staffelführer
15	Oberstammführer	Oberarbeitsführer	Stabsoberführerin	NSKK-Oberstaffelführer
16	Bannführer	Oberstarbeitsführer	Stabshauptführerin	NSKK-Standartenführer
	Oberbannführer			NSKK-Oberführer
17	Hauptbannführer	Generalarbeitsführer		NSKK-Brigadeführer
18	Gebietsführer	Obergeneralarbeitsführer		NSKK-Gruppenführer
19	Obergebietsführer			NSKK-Obergruppenführer
20	Stabsführer der Reichs-jugendführung			
21	Reichsjugendführer	Reichsarbeitsführer		NSKK-Korpsführer
22				

#	NSFK	RLB	TeNo	Organisation Todt
1	NSFK-Mann	Truppmann	Anwärter der TN	OT-Arbeiter
2	NSFK-Sturmmann			OT-Vorarbeiter
3	NSFK-Rottenführer	Obertruppmann	Unterwachtmeister d.TN	OT-Meister
				OT-Obermeister
4	NSFK-Scharführer	Truppwart	Rottwachtmeister d.TN	OT-Bauführer
5	NSKK-Oberscharführer	Obertruppwart	Wachtmeister d.TN	OT-Oberbauführer
				OT-Hauptbauführer
6			Oberwachtmeister d.TN	
7	NSFK-Truppführer	Truppmeister	Zugwachtmeister d.TN	OT-Truppführer
8	NSKK-Obertruppführer	Obertruppmeister		OT-Obertruppführer
9			Hauptwachtmeister d.TN	
10			Bereitschaftsleiter d.TN	
			Meister der TeNo	
11	NSFK-Sturmführer	Führer	Zugführer der TeNo	OT-Haupttruppführer
12	NSFK-Obersturmführer	Oberführer	Oberzugführer d.TN	OT-Bauleiter
13	NSFK-Hauptsturmführer	Hauptführer	Bereitschaftsführer d.TN	OT-Oberbauleiter
14	NSFK-Sturmbannführer		Abteilungsführer d.TN	OT-Hauptbauleiter
15	NSFK-Obersturmbannführer		Oberabteilungsführer der TeNo	OT-Einsatzleiter
16	NSFK-Standartenführer		Landesführer d.TN	OT-Einsatzgruppenleiter II
	NSFK-Oberführer			
17	NSFK-Brigadeführer		Stellv. Reichsführer der TeNo	
18	NSFK-Gruppenführer	Gruppenführer	Reichsführer d.TeNo	
19	NSFK-Obergruppenführer	Vize-Präsident		OT-Einsatzgruppenleiter I
20				Chef des Amtes Bau
21	NSFK-Korpsführer	RLB-Präsident		OT
22				

	DRK Males	DRK Females	Stahlhelm	SHD	Bahnschutzpolizei
1	DRK-Anwärter	DRK-Anwärterin	Wehrmann	SHD-Mann	Bzp.Anwärter
2					Bzp.Mann
3	DRK-Helfer	DRK-Helferin	Oberwehrmann		Bzp.Stellvertreter-Gruppenführer
4	Vorhelfer	DRK Vorhelferin		Truppführer	Bzp.Gruppenführer
5	Vorhelfer mit Gruppenführerprüfung		Stabswehrmann		Bzp.Obergruppenführer
6					
7	Oberhelfer	DRK-Oberhelferin	Gruppenführer	Gruppenführer	Bzp.Unterzugführer
8	Oberhelfer mit Zugführerprüfung		Feldmeister	Hauptgruppenführer	Bzp.Zugführer
9					
10	Haupthelfer	DRK-Haupthelferin	Oberfeldmeister	Stabsgruppenführer	Bzp.Oberzugführer
11	Wachtführer	DRK-Wachtführerin	Zugführer	Zugführer	Bzp.Abteilungsführer
12	Oberwachtführer	DRK-Oberwachtführerin	Oberzugführer	Oberzugführer	Bzp.Oberabteilungsführer
13	Hauptführer	DRK-Hauptführerin	Kompanieführer	Bereitschaftsführer	Bzp.Abteilungshauptführer
14	Feldführer	DRK-Feldführerin	Battaillonsführer	Abteilungsführer	Bzp.Bezirksführer
15	Oberfeldführer	DRK-Oberfeldführerin	Stabsführer	Abteilungsleiter	Bzp.Berzirkshauptführer
16	Oberstführer	DRK-Oberstführerin	Regimentsführer		Stabsführer der Bzp.
17	Generalführer	DRK-Generalführerin	Brigadeführer		Chef der Bzp.
18	Generalhauptführer	DRK-Generalhauptführerin	Divisionsführer		
19			Obergruppenführer		
20			Bundeshauptmann		
21			Bundesführer		
22					

AD	Allgemeinedienst (General service)
AHS	Adolf Hitler Schulen (Adolf Hitler Schools)
AO	Auslandsorganisation (Overseas organisation)
BD	Bereitschaftsdienst (Stand-by duty)
BDM	Bund Deutsche Mädel (League of German Girls)
DAF	Deutsche Arbeitsfront (German Labour Front)
DFO	Deutsche Falken Orden (German Falconry Order)
DJ (1)	Deutsche Jungvolk (Junior Division of the Hitler Youth)
DJ (2)	Deutsche Jägerschaft (German Hunting Association)
DLV	Deutsch Luftschutzverband (German Air-raid Protection Association)
FJK	Feldjägerkorps (Military Police)
HJ	Hitlerjugend (Hitler Youth)
KfHB	Kyffhäuserbund (Veterans organisation)
LAH	Leibstandart Adolf Hitler (SS Bodyguard Regiment, later a full SS Division)
LD	Luftschutzdienst (Air-raid Protection Service)
LSW	Luftschutz Warndienst (Air-raid Warning Service)
NAPOLA	See NPEA
NPEA	Nationalpolitische Erziehungsanstalt (National Political Educational Establishment)
NS	Nationalsozialist (National Socialist)
NSBO	NS Betriebsorganisation (NS Factory Organisation)
NSFK	NS Fliegerkorps (NS Flying Corps)
NSHAGO	NS Handels und Gewerbeorganisation (NS Trade and Industry Organisation)
NSKK	NS Kraftfahrkorps (NS Motor Corps)
NSKOV	NS Kriegsopferversorgung (NS War Victims Welfare Organisation)
NS-RKB	NS Reichskriegerbund (NS War Veterans Association)
OT	Organisation Todt
RAB	Reichsautobahn
RAD	Reichs Arbeitsdienst (German Labour Service)
RADwJ	Reichs Arbeitsdienst der weiblichen Jugend (Female youth branch of the Labour Service)
RJF	Reichs Jugendführer (German Youth Leader)
RLB	Reichsluftschutzbund (German Air-raid Protection Association)
RMBO	Reichsministerium für die besetzten Ostgebiete (Ministry for the occupied Eastern Territories)
SA	Sturmabteilung (Storm Troops)
SD	Sicherheitsdienst (Security Service)
SHD	Sicherheits und Hilfsdienst (Safety and Aid Service)
SP	Transportkorps 'Speer'
SS	Schutzstaffel
SS-VT	SS Verfügungstruppe (SS Special Purpose Troops)
TeNo	Technische Nothilfe (Technical Emergency Help)
TD	Technischedienst (Technical Service)
VT	Verfügunstruppe (Special Purpose Troops)
Waffen-SS	Armed SS